# Bringing Linguistics ir
# Spanish Language Cla

*Bringing Linguistics into the Spanish Language Classroom* is a practical, time-saving resource that allows teachers to easily integrate the most interesting and important findings of Hispanic linguistics into their Spanish language classes.

Teachers will find classroom-ready explanations and PowerPoint slides for each topic covered, as well as instructions and materials for in-class activities and take-home projects that will engage students in this fresh take on the target language. Slide presentations for each chapter are available online at www.routledge.com/9780367111960.

The book covers aspects of Spanish from the trilled *r* to the personal *a*, from Indo-European origins to modern dialects, and from children's first words to adult speech errors. An innovative set of five essential linguistics-based questions organizes and contextualizes this wide range of material:

1 How is Spanish different from other languages?
2 How is Spanish similar to other languages?
3 What are the roots of Spanish?
4 How does Spanish vary?
5 How do people learn and use Spanish?

Fully customizable to teacher and student interest, proficiency level, and time available in class, this book is ideal for Spanish language teachers looking to incorporate valuable linguistic insights into their curricula, even if they lack prior knowledge of this field. It is an excellent resource for Hispanic linguistics courses as well.

**Judy Hochberg** has a PhD in Linguistics from Stanford University and teaches Spanish at Fordham University, New York. She is the author of *¿Por qué? 101 Questions about Spanish* (2016) and blogs at spanishlinguist.us.

# Bringing Linguistics into the Spanish Language Classroom

A Teacher's Guide

Judy Hochberg

Spanish List Advisor: Javier Muñoz-Basols

 Routledge
Taylor & Francis Group

LONDON AND NEW YORK

First published 2021
by Routledge
2 Park Square, Milton Park, Abingdon, Oxon OX14 4RN

and by Routledge
52 Vanderbilt Avenue, New York, NY 10017

*Routledge is an imprint of the Taylor & Francis Group, an informa business*

*British Library Cataloguing-in-Publication Data*
A catalogue record for this book is available from the British Library

*Library of Congress Cataloging-in-Publication Data*
Names: Hochberg, Judith Golden, author.
Title: Bringing linguistics into the Spanish language classroom:
a teacher's guide / Judy Hochberg.
Description: Abingdon, Oxon; New York, NY: Routledge, 2021. |
Includes bibliographical references and index.
Identifiers: LCCN 2020045024 (print) | LCCN 2020045025 (ebook) |
ISBN 9780367111946 (hardback) | ISBN 9780367111960 (paperback) |
ISBN 9780429025228 (ebook)
Subjects: LCSH: Spanish language—Study and teaching. |
Applied linguistics.
Classification: LCC PC4065 .H63 2021 (print) |
LCC PC4065 (ebook) | DDC 468.0071—dc23
LC record available at https://lccn.loc.gov/2020045024
LC ebook record available at https://lccn.loc.gov/2020045025

ISBN: 978-0-367-11194-6 (hbk)
ISBN: 978-0-367-11196-0 (pbk)
ISBN: 978-0-429-02522-8 (ebk)

Typeset in Times New Roman
by codeMantra

Access the Support Material: www.routledge.com/9780367111960

For my students
*A mis estudiantes*

# Contents

# Preface

This book unites two strands of my career as a linguist and Spanish teacher. The first strand dates from the teacher training classes I took at Pace University in the aughts. When we learned about essential questions as a key ingredient in curriculum design, I was disappointed that there did not seem to be an adequate set of questions for world languages. It struck me as axiomatic that these should come from the field of linguistics.

The second strand dates from the publication of my first book, *¿Por qué? 101 Questions about Spanish*, in 2016. I learned so many exciting things about Spanish over the course of writing the book that I was driven to further share this knowledge. I was sure that it would be interesting and useful for teachers and their students. Over the next few years I therefore developed a presentation, which I gave at several conferences for language teachers, on how to bring such linguistic insights into the language classroom in general and the Spanish language classroom in particular.

As I worked with this material, to my delight a sensible set of five essential questions emerged, based on the various subfields of linguistics, that nicely encompassed all of the 101 topics I had explored in my book as well as others I had come across in the intervening years. Moreover, these questions were general enough to apply to the teaching of other languages as well. This book's Introduction presents these essential questions as they apply to Spanish, and its five chapters take them up in turn. I hope that teachers of other languages will attempt to apply these questions to their own target languages in the future.

Many Spanish teachers have taken a required course or two on Hispanic linguistics, but these classes rarely address how best to incorporate this perspective into classroom practice. Besides offering the essential questions as an overarching structure, this book bridges the gap between theory and practice with specific explanations, activities, assignments, and even PowerPoint slides that teachers can use in their own classrooms. I hope that readers will find this approach as fruitful as I have.

# Acknowledgments

Several colleagues helped me develop the five essential questions that organize this book. Jay McTighe shared with me his own ongoing list of essential questions for language teaching and discussed my more linguistically oriented ideas. He, Lori Langer de Ramirez, and anonymous reviewers gave valuable feedback on my article "Essential questions for linguistic literacy in the world language classroom," published in the *NECTFL Review* in September 2019, part of which I have revised as part of this book's Introduction. Marianne Washburn, Alessia Valfredini, Wendy Witt, and Maria Licia Sotgiu explored with me the possible application of the essential questions to their own target languages.

Daniel Nappo, of the University of Tennessee, and Susan Ranft, formerly of Niles North High School, encouraged me to trust that Spanish teachers who were not linguists would find value in this book's approach. Daniel offered perspicacious comments on a first draft. Prof. Ana Blanco Canalas, of the Universidad de Alcalá, helped me to better understand her data on -*s* deletion. An anonymous reviewer provided helpful feedback and caught some Spanish mistakes, though no doubt others remain.

My family, especially my husband, encouraged me in this project and patiently shared me with it, especially during the all-absorbing last lap. My son Aaron constructively critiqued my writing, and my grandson Oscar helped me with an evasive citation.

Rosie McEwan, my editor at Routledge, saw the book's potential and stuck with me even when distraction, a move, and a pandemic postponed its completion.

I am grateful to the many organizations around the Spanish-speaking world that granted me permission to reproduce their intellectual property. In the United States: the *NECTFL Review*, as mentioned above, and the National Academy of Sciences, for an illustration of the *b/v* contrast that Spanish-speaking infants learn to ignore (Slide 5.5). In Puerto Rico: Ediciones Callejón, for Magali García Ramis's description of the affective value of the Puerto Rican *r* (Slide 4.64). In Spain: Europa Press, for Hugo Chávez's humorous reaction to the loss of the letter *ch* (Slide 1.14); *El País*, for Gabriel García Márquez's brilliant defense of the *eñe* (Slide 1.28); Fundación Biblioteca Virtual Miguel de Cervantes, for a teacher's description of students who avoid using *por* and *para* (Slide 5.15); and Juegosdepalabras.com, for an impressive list of *palabras panvocálicas* (Slide 2.6). In Argentina: *Revista Fonoaudiológica*, for MRIs of tongue positions (Slide 2.5). In Costa Rica: *La Nación*, for Hugo Mora Poltronieri's impassioned defense of *voseo* (Slide 4.78).

Four images in the slide presentations that accompany this book were published under some version of the Creative Commons Attribution license, which allows users to adapt and share their work as long as they give appropriate credit, provide a link to the license, and indicate if changes were made.

- Helmbrecht 2013 (map of formal and informal subject pronouns, Slide 2.19), https://wals.info/feature/45A#1/23/149. The version in the slide is cropped to focus on Western Europe.
- Dahl and Velupillai 2013 (map of perfective/imperfective aspect, Slide 2.28), https://wals.info/feature/65A#1/27/149. The version in the slide is cropped to remove extraneous landmasses.
- Koppchen 2012 (tiled bench in Santa Cruz de Tenerife, Slide 3.35), https://commons.wikimedia.org/wiki/File:Patos_19.jpg. The version in the slide is cropped to focus on a small set of tiles.
- Tataryn 2012 (map of Roman Empire, Slides 3.26 and 3.27), https://commons.wikimedia.org/wiki/File:Roman_Empire_Trajan_117AD-pt.svg. The version in Slide 3.27 was altered by removing all boundaries, rivers, and place names.

Six images were published under some version of the Creative Commons Attribution-Share Alike license, which additionally requires users to distribute any altered version of an image under the same license. Of these images, this additional requirement applies to Hayden et al. (2015), OtterAM (2015), and Vigo (2009), for which I hereby grant such license.

- Beltz 2005 (*bota* 'wineskin,' Slides 3.18, 3.19, and 3.23), https://commons.wikimedia.org/wiki/File:Bota_de_vino.jpg.
- García 2006 (Dama del Elche, Slide 3.17), https://commons.wikimedia.org/wiki/File:Dama_de_Elche_(M.A.N._Madrid)_01.jpg.
- Hayden, G. Balakhadze, Flappiefh, and Alphathon 2015 (map of Indo-European language family, Slide 3.5), commons.wikimedia.org/wiki/File:Indo-European_branches_map.svg. A red star was added to indicate the likely point of origin of the language family.
- Mediatus 2010 (graffiti from Pompeii, Slide 3.28), https://commons.wikimedia.org/wiki/File:Pompei,_Gladiatoren,_AE_1914,_00157.jpg.

- OtterAM 2015 (*lúcuma* 'eggfruit,' Slide 2.35), https://commons.wikimedia. org/wiki/index.php?curid=42752568. The image is cropped to focus on a single fruit.
- Vigo 2009 (animation of spread of Castellano, Slide 3.40), https:// commons.wikimedia.org/wiki/File:Linguistic_map_Southwestern_ Europe-en.gif. The animation is slowed down.

In addition, all maps created with mapchart.net are hereby licensed under a Creative Commons Attribution-ShareAlike 4.0 International License.

# Introduction

## Why linguistics?

The field of Hispanic linguistics sheds light on aspects of Spanish from phonology to grammar, from history to dialectology, and from acquisition to adult cognition. Some examples are the following:

- Spanish is one of the few languages that use a single preposition (*en*) to express the meanings 'in' and 'on.'
- Grammatical gender is not only a core feature of Spanish and other Romance languages but is found in many unrelated languages worldwide.
- *Ser* and *ir* are irregular, in part, because they each combine three distinct historical verb roots.
- Some Latin American dialects have absorbed pronunciation patterns and/or grammatical features from indigenous languages.
- It takes many children at least six years to master the trilled *r*.

Spanish teachers already strive to lead their students toward functional competence in the language and an appreciation of Hispanic culture. However, even if they meet both these goals their students are likely to miss out on the perspectives that linguistics can offer. Teachers may have had some training in Hispanic linguistics but not in how best to apply it. This book bridges that gap, enabling Spanish teachers to enrich their practice with insights from this allied field.

Linguistic insights can contribute to Spanish instruction in three ways. First and foremost, they add intellectual interest to the classroom by connecting Spanish to other languages, to general linguistic principles, and to other fields such as history, geography, sociology, and psychology. Second, they can help students better understand and master genuinely challenging aspects of Spanish, such as irregular verbs. Finally, students may be more willing to accept differences between Spanish and their native language (presumably English) if they learn that these differences are shared by other languages, or, conversely, that they are distinctive or even unique features of Spanish.

The five examples listed above correspond to five essential questions that provide this book's organizing framework:

1    How is Spanish different from other languages?
2    How is Spanish similar to other languages?
3    What are the roots of Spanish?
4    How does Spanish vary?
5    How do people learn and use Spanish?

Or, *en español*:

1    *¿En qué se diferencia el español de otros idiomas?*
2    *¿Cómo se parece el español a otros idiomas?*
3    *¿Cuáles son las raíces del español?*
4    *¿Cómo varía el español?*
5    *¿Cómo se aprende y se usa el español?*

For a discussion of the essential questions approach in general, how these questions exemplify this approach, and their close connection to the field of linguistics, see the section "More about the essential questions" later in this Introduction.

## How to use this book

Each chapter of this book covers several topics relevant to one of the essential questions, as summarized in Table 1. Crucially, the chapters provide

*Table 1* Essential questions and topics

| Essential question | Scope of topics |
|---|---|
| 1 How is Spanish different from other languages? | Spanish as a major world language. Unique or unusual features of the written language, phonology, vocabulary, and grammar. |
| 2 How is Spanish similar to other languages? | Features of Spanish that are shared by many other languages, including aspects of the written language, phonology, vocabulary, and grammar. |
| 3 What are the roots of Spanish? | External history: a series of conquests, from Indo-European to the Americas. Internal history: changes in phonology, vocabulary, and grammar. |
| 4 How does Spanish vary? | Dialects, multilingualism, and code-switching. Geographic and social variation in phonology, vocabulary, and grammar. |
| 5 How do people learn and use Spanish? | How children learn phonology, vocabulary, and grammar. Second language acquisition. Evidence pertinent to language processing from speech errors, language and thought, and language games (*jerigonzas*). |

instructors with everything they need to incorporate these topics into their teaching. Teachers can choose which topics to share with their classes and to what degree, as discussed further below.

The presentation of each topic begins with a brief explanation in English ("Just the facts") and an even briefer one in simple Spanish ("Teacher talk"). These explanations use a minimum of linguistic terminology and resort to phonetic notation only when it is difficult to represent sounds with English or Spanish spelling (e.g. "/ʒ/ as in *pleasure*"). Spanish words in the text are generally included without translations.

After these two explanations, the reader will find instructions for in-class activities and take-home projects that motivate, teach, reinforce, or explore the topic. Tables 2 and 3 list and exemplify the types of activities and projects included. Appendices A and B list all 128 activities and 67 projects,

*Table 2* Types of in-class activities

| Type | Number of activities | Example |
|---|---|---|
| Activate knowledge | 21 | Using general knowledge, identify and rank the top five Spanish-speaking countries and estimate their Spanish-speaking populations. |
| Analyze | 23 | Analyze children's early conjugation errors. |
| Categorize | 6 | Divide words that Spanish borrowed from Arabic into a provided set of semantic categories (*arquitectura, ciencias*, etc.) |
| Create | 20 | Invent a business and decide between *tú* and *usted* as the best choice for wording on its website. |
| Debate | 4 | Debate the value of the inverted ¿ and ¡ marks. Should English adopt them? |
| Discuss | 8 | Discuss why a speaker's age, gender, and other factors affect their adoption of dialectal features, such as final -s deletion. |
| Listen | 9 | Identify speakers' likely origins based on their pronunciation of words like *yo* and *calle*. |
| Practice | 9 | Practice tongue twisters while using different pronunciation styles: *seseo, ceceo*, and the *s/th* distinction. |
| Read and discuss | 12 | Read a defense of *voseo* from a Costa Rican newspaper and, besides analyzing the text, discuss the relationship it invokes between language use and cultural identity. |
| See and discuss | 12 | Discuss the meaning of a painting in the collection of New York's Museum of Modern Art that depicts a gigantic Ñ. |
| Watch and discuss | 5 | Watch a Bolivian TV news report about the 2015 reinstallation of Evo Morales as president, discuss it with classmates, and summarize it in a paragraph using the *pretérito* and *imperfecto*. |

*Table 3* Types of take-home projects

| Type | Number of projects | Example |
|---|---|---|
| Ask a native speaker | 10 | Ask a native speaker about unique vocabulary used in their country. |
| Collect and analyze data | 7 | Look up the origins of words from a semantic domain, such as clothing terms. |
| Create | 9 | Design a class logo that incorporates the tilde. |
| Find examples | 7 | On Forvo.com identify varying pronunciations of a word like *yo* or *calle* as recorded by speakers from Spain, Argentina, and other countries. |
| Look up items | 12 | Use the Real Academia Española dictionary to identify the gender and origin (Greek or not Greek) of several words ending in *-ma*. |
| Research | 6 | Compare the *catalán/castellano* conflict to another language conflict. |
| Profile | 9 | Profile a minority language of Spain, creating a poster or presentation. |
| Try something new | 4 | Try a sample Spanish lesson using software of your choice, and compare it with our in-class instruction. |
| WebQuest | 3 | Use Internet resources to answer questions about the history and current status of indigenous Latin American languages. |

indicating the type of each one (as in Tables 2 and 3) and also its suitability for different levels of instruction.

Many of the activities and projects essentially reverse-engineer information presented earlier. For example, the "Just the facts" section for the topic "Multilingualism in Latin America" refers to Slide 4.31, a map of the twenty most-spoken indigenous languages of Latin America. In the take-home project "Map the most-spoken indigenous languages" students look up and map these languages for themselves. Teachers should be aware of these parallels and avoid presenting material in class that reveals the answers to an activity or project they plan to assign.

Some activities can be done at home instead of in class. These are noted in the text and marked with an asterisk (*) in Appendix A. In addition, some take-home projects supplement or replace corresponding in-class activities. For example, the PowerPoint slide for the Chapter 4 in-class activity "Listen to indigenous languages" contains links to videos of speakers of several indigenous languages, but in the take-home project "Find a video of an indigenous language" students provide such videos themselves. These activities and projects are noted in the text and marked with a double asterisk (**) in Appendices A and B.

As shown in Table 3, several take-home projects have students "ask a native speaker" about some topic. These projects revolve around features of Spanish that native speakers are likely to be familiar with and find interesting, such as dialectal vocabulary, second person pronouns, and children's early verb conjugation errors. Teachers who plan to assign one or more of these projects should have students identify a native speaker partner early in the course. Students might be able to find a partner in their school or even in their family. If not, they should reach out via social media, or through websites for finding pen pals individually or on a class-wide basis.

Teachers can adapt many of the book's activities and projects for multiple levels of instruction. The Chapter 1 activity "Rank the top five Spanish-speaking countries" is a good example. Beginning students can carry it out using simple sentences like *México no es dos, es uno* that require little more than numbers and a few basic words. For advanced students, the same activity can be an opportunity to practice complex sentences and verb tenses, as in *México tendrá más hispanohablantes que España* or *Dudo que Puerto Rico tenga más hispanohablantes que Cuba*. As another example, students can carry out "Ask a native speaker" projects in either English or Spanish.

Each chapter has a corresponding PowerPoint presentation that is available online; Appendix C lists each chapter's slides. Some slides help teachers present the topics in their chapter. The materials in these slides include explanations and descriptions, diagrams, word lists, sample data from research studies, maps, quotations, images, and links to other images as well as articles and videos. Other slides contain instructions and supporting materials for in-class activities and take-home projects. The slides are in Spanish except for an occasional English translation; several include illustrations for non-basic vocabulary to help the instructor sidestep English explanations.

Each chapter closes with a list of references that apply to the chapter's text and also its slide presentation.

The approach presented in this book is highly customizable: teachers can adopt it to different degrees depending on their own interest, their students' interests and level of maturity, and, of course, the time available. As a simplification, teachers can adopt this approach to a minimal, moderate, or maximal degree.

- At a **minimum**, teachers can incorporate into their existing curricula the linguistic insights that they judge to have the most practical value and/or general interest. As an example of the former, teachers can use the diagram in Slide 3.82 to explain the origin of present-tense stem-changing verbs like *perder* and *poder*. As an example of the latter, students can observe in Slide 4.41 the dramatic difference between the survival of indigenous American languages in Latin America and the United States. Slides most likely to be of interest to such teachers are in boldface in Appendix C.

- At a **moderate** level, teachers can also include the in-class activities and take-home projects that they judge to have the most practical value and/ or general interest. As an example of the former, a teacher might have half the students in a beginning class wear a tie to highlight the difference between *tú* and *usted,* as described in Chapter 1. As an example of the latter, students in an advanced class might read and discuss Gabriel García Márquez's defense of the *eñe* (Slide 1.28). Activities and projects most likely to be of interest to such teachers are in boldface in Appendices A and B.
- A teacher who takes a **maximal** dive into this approach should present the five essential questions at the beginning of a course. During the course the class should cover some topics within the scope of all five questions, doing at least one in-class activity or take-home project for each of these topics. The class could maintain a poster, or electronic document, of the essential questions, which they flesh out during the course as they study each topic. They will end up with something akin to this book's table of contents.

The following section will be of greatest interest to teachers who opt for the maximal option.

## More about the essential questions

"Essential questions" – challenging, open-ended questions that provide focus and intellectual depth for a course or unit – have been a staple of curriculum design since Wiggins and McTighe introduced them in *Understanding by Design* (1998). In a follow-up publication, McTighe and Wiggin offered examples of essential questions from various disciplines, including world language (2013, 3). They presented questions about learning the target language (e.g., "How can I sound more like a native speaker?") and also its culture (e.g., "How can I explore and describe cultures without stereotyping them?"). These are important questions, but they do not sufficiently address the object of acquisition: the target language itself.

The field of linguistics offers a robust framework for generating target language-oriented essential questions for language learning. As a preliminary, one can identify five essential questions for linguistics itself, each based on one of its subfields:

1 *How are languages different?* In the core field of descriptive linguistics, linguists explore the full range of the tools that languages can draw on: different sounds, meanings, and grammatical encodings.
2 *How are languages similar?* The search for universals is perhaps the central goal of theoretical linguistics. It is connected to the practical aim of designing computer systems that can be tuned or trained to process a variety of languages.

3   *How are languages related?* The subfield of historical linguistics establishes family trees among languages and also examines how languages interact and influence each other.

4   *How do social and other factors affect language use?* Language is not spoken in a vacuum. The subfield of sociolinguistics investigates variations in language use due to geography, class, sex, age, and communicative context.

5   *How do people learn and process languages?* The subfield of psycholinguistics covers first and second language acquisition and also how speakers produce and understand language.

The five essential questions for the Spanish language classroom that form the framework for this book directly parallel these questions for linguistics. Of course, one could rework them for any other language (e.g. "How is Hebrew different from other languages?" or "How do people learn and use Swahili?") or for target languages in general.

Many features of Spanish can be viewed through the lens of one or more of these questions. The past tense is a good example because it relates to all five. Compared to most other languages, Spanish actively uses a greater variety of constructions (conjugations and auxiliary structures) to express the past (Question 1). As in other languages, frequent verbs like *ir* and *ser* are the most likely to be irregular in the past tense as well as other tenses (Question 2). The roots of Spanish explain specific irregularities such as the identical preterite forms of *ir* and *ser* (Question 3). If less educated, or when speaking informally, many speakers add an *s* to the second person singular form of the preterite, e.g. *\*hablastes* for *hablaste*, because this is the only such form that lacks an *-s* (Question 4). Finally, children's errors as they learn the past tense, such as *\*saló* for *salió*, resemble those of students learning Spanish as a second language (Question 5). These topics are all covered in their respective chapters.

The five questions in this book meet McTighe and Wiggins's various criteria for essential questions (2013, 3). For example, they are open-ended, without a "single, final, and correct answer." While each one of these questions can be contemplated by a beginning Spanish student, a full answer would require at least a book-length treatment. In addition, they "recur over time." Since the questions are not specific to one aspect of Spanish, students can revisit them during a semester, a year, or even a longer course of study. As a final example, they point toward "important, transferable ideas." The questions can be applied to other target languages, and also connect language study with history (Question 3), sociology (Question 4), and psychology (Question 5).

Note that Questions 3–5 are thus relevant to ACTFL's (2012) "Connections" World-Readiness Standard ("Learners build, reinforce, and expand their knowledge of other disciplines"). At the same time, Questions 1 and 2 provide a principled way to address the "Comparisons" standard ("Learners use the language to investigate, explain, and reflect on the nature of language through comparisons of the language studied and their own"). The connection between these essential questions and the ACTFL standards underscores their potential value to all Spanish teachers.

## References

American Council on the Teaching of Foreign Languages. 2012. *ACTFL proficiency guidelines.* Retrieved from https://www.actfl.org/publications/guidelines-and-manuals/actfl-proficiency-guidelines-2012.

McTighe, J., and G. Wiggins. 2013. *Essential questions: Opening doors to student understanding.* Alexandria, VA: ASCD.

Wiggins, G., and J. McTighe. 1998. *Understanding by design.* Alexandria, VA: ASCD.

# Chapter I

# How is Spanish different from other languages?

This chapter describes features of Spanish that are unusual or even unique among the languages of the world. Knowing what sets Spanish apart from other languages can help motivate students. This is especially important for features that students tend to neglect, such as the inverted ¿ and ¡ questions marks, or that pose a learning challenge, such as the many past tenses of Spanish. Essentially, while these features may be a nuisance for students, they help to make Spanish special.

The chapter begins with the status of Spanish as a major world language, surely one of the language's most unusual features, then moves on to specific aspects of the language. As in later chapters, these run the gamut from Spanish writing to phonology, vocabulary, and grammar. The inverted marks and the past tenses are examples of writing and grammar. In terms of phonology, the Castilian *th* is an example of an unusual sound, while in terms of vocabulary, the preposition *en* is unusual because its meaning is so broad.

Some of the in-class activities and take-home projects for this chapter ask students to **celebrate** a feature of Spanish: making word clouds of words with an *eñe*, for instance, or plotting on a map the home countries of the eleven Spanish-speaking Nobel laureates in literature. Others give students the chance to **explore** a feature in more depth: for example, learning about the Real Academia Española (RAE) from the institution's own videos, or considering how some authors exploit the contrast between the *-ra* and *-se* imperfect subjunctives. Some delve into **history**: for example, using open-access Internet software to track the growing ascendancy of the *-ra* imperfect subjunctive, or witnessing the origins of the tilde in Christopher Columbus's letter about his first voyage. Finally, some activities and projects ask students to **engage** with a linguistic feature: for example, debating the value of the inverted marks, or trying to use all of Spanish's many past tenses in a summary of a story or video. For a full list of the chapter's activities and projects, and their suitability for different levels of instruction, see Appendices A and B.

Later chapters explore two other unusual features of Spanish: the development of its language standard through conquest rather than cultural dominance ("The Reconquista," in Chapter 3) and the psychological impact of the "se *accidental*" ("Language and Thought," in Chapter 5).

## Spanish in the world

### Speakers and countries

*Just the facts*

Spanish is a major world language. It is ranked second worldwide in its number of first-language speakers, after Chinese and ahead of English (Slide 1.1, based on Eberhard, Simons, and Fennig 2020). It is an official language in twenty-one countries in five continents: the three Americas (South, Central, and North), Europe, and Africa (Slide 1.2).

*Teacher talk*

"El español es el segundo idioma más hablado del mundo, después del chino y antes del inglés. También es un idioma oficial en veintiún países en cinco continentes: Europa, África y las tres Américas."

*In-class activities*

As described in the Introduction, teachers can adapt the first two activities to a range of Spanish abilities.

* **Rank Spanish among the world's top languages.** The teacher displays a list of the world's ten most widely spoken languages, shown in alphabetical order in Slide 1.3. Student pairs or groups estimate which language has the most speakers, which the second most, and so on down to ten. To incorporate practice of higher numbers, students can also estimate each language's number of speakers. Students then report their estimated rankings (and populations) for each language, with a volunteer recording them on the board. At this point student estimates can be compared with the actual rankings and numbers of speakers in Slide 1.1.
* **Rank the top five Spanish-speaking countries.** Student pairs or groups write down, in order, which they believe are the five Spanish-speaking countries with the most first-language Spanish speakers. They can do this with or without reference to the list of Spanish-speaking countries in Slide 1.4. As in the previous activity, to incorporate practice of higher numbers, students can also estimate the number of first-language Spanish speakers in each of their designated top five countries. Again as in the previous activity, students report their proposed rankings (and populations) as a volunteer records these on the board; the class then

compares them with the actual top five countries in Slide 1.5 (based on Eberhard, Simons, and Fennig 2020).

Afterward, the class can discuss any surprises in these data. For example, in the author's experience many students assume that Puerto Rico is in the top five, but almost all overlook Colombia. They are also impressed that the United States makes the top five. If a list of Spanish-speaking countries is not provided as in Slide 1.4, students may include Brazil.

- **Map Spanish-speaking countries by name and population size.** For this activity, each pair or group of students needs a copy of the outline map in Slide 1.6, which includes all Spanish-speaking countries as well as their neighboring countries in the Americas, Europe, and Africa. Working from the list of countries in Slide 1.7, and referring to a labeled map as needed, students then add country names to their map (most names will fit in the oceans) and color-code the countries according to their number of first-language Spanish speakers. The colors in Slide 1.7 designate different ranges of population size; for example, the countries in green have fewer than a million such speakers. Students can use these colors or choose their own – or, for that matter, different population ranges.

  As in the previous activity, the class can then discuss any surprises in the data. Teachers can also point out that many residents of Spain, Guatemala, Peru, Bolivia, and Paraguay are excluded from the data in Slide 1.7 because they speak a language other than Spanish as a first language (see Chapter 4).

## Take-home project

- **Profile a Spanish-speaking country.** Each student chooses or is assigned a Spanish-speaking country to profile. If there are more students than countries, students can work in pairs; if there are more countries than students, the teacher or students can decide which to include in the project. Using resources such as the CIA World Factbook, Ethnologue (if students have access through their school), or Wikipedia (if school policy allows), each student creates a language profile of his or her assigned country that includes the information shown in Slide 1.8. The profile may be in the form of a poster, slide presentation, or oral report that can be shared with the class.

## The Academy system

### Just the facts

Spanish has a worldwide institutional presence. Each Spanish-speaking country, including the United States and the Philippines, has an official Spanish language Academy; together, the twenty-three Academies form the

Asociación de Academias de la Lengua Española (ASALE). ASALE publishes popular books including various grammars, dictionaries, and a spelling guide. Both laypeople and scholars use its online resources, including a dictionary maintained by the Real Academia Española (Spain's original Academy). ASALE holds periodic conferences at which representatives from each country vote on issues such as spelling reform and new vocabulary.

*Teacher talk*

"Cada país de habla española, incluso los Estados Unidos, tiene una 'Academia' que estudia y mantiene el idioma. La Asociación de Academias de la Lengua Española publica diccionarios y otros libros, y decide cuestiones como la aceptación de nuevo vocabulario y los cambios ortográficos."

*In-class activities*

- **Learn from videos about the Real Academia Española.** Slides 1.9 and 1.10 contain links to two introductory videos from the Real Academia Española; Spanish subtitles are available. These slides also contain a list of possible comprehension questions based on the videos.
- **Debate the Real Academia Española.** Hold a class debate on one of the topics in Slide 1.11.
- **Discuss the elimination of *ch* and *ll*.** A recent example of the power of the Academy system was the 1994 decision to eliminate *ch* and *ll* as distinct "letters" of the Spanish alphabet (technically, digraphs or *dígrafos*). This change was instigated by Spain's Real Academia Española, adopted by a majority vote of the ASALE members in 1994, and fully implemented in 2010. Students can read the Academia's summary of the change (Slide 1.12, from RAE 2010) and discuss its advantages and disadvantages (a possible list is in Slide 1.13). Slide 1.14 relays a humorous reaction to the elimination of *ch* from the late Hugo Chávez, the former president of Venezuela (Notimérica 2010). The class should try to explain his joke, which relies on a deliberate misunderstanding of the RAE's change in the alphabet.

*Take-home projects*

- **Profile a Spanish language Academy.** Each student chooses or is assigned a Spanish-speaking country; the United States should be included. If there are more students than countries, students can work in pairs; if there are more countries than students, the teacher or students can decide which to include in the project. Each student then profiles the Spanish language Academy of his or her assigned country, using the information on the ASALE website (asale.org) and the Academy's own website (the relevant

URLs can be found on asale.org). A profile should include the information shown in Slide 1.15 and can be in the form of a poster, slide presentation, or oral report that can be shared with the class.

As a possible in-class follow-up, students can work in groups to compare their Academies' characteristics and activities, then summarize and present their findings to the class. This can be combined with a review of question words (*cuántos, qué* vs. *cuál*, and so on) by having students first prepare questions to ask each other about their Academies.

- **Profile an Academy's members.** As in the previous project, each student (or pair of students) chooses or is assigned a country's Spanish language Academy. Each Academy's website has a list of its members and some information about them, including that shown in Slide 1.16. Students can summarize this information in whatever way the teacher prefers: in a table, a series of pie charts, an infographic...Information from students' individual academies can also be combined to give a composite picture of Spanish language academicians.
- **Prepare interview questions for an Academy member.** Each student prepares a list of interview questions that he or she would like to ask a member of a Spanish language Academy. These could be generic or aimed at a specific Academy or Academy member.

### The Nobel Prize in Literature

*Just the facts*

Eleven writers from six Spanish-speaking countries in four continents have won the Nobel Prize for Literature (Slide 1.17). This is another measure of the international scope of Spanish.

*Teacher talk*

"Once escritores de seis países hispanos, en cuatro continentes, han ganado el Premio Nobel de Literatura. Es otra prueba de la importancia mundial del español."

*In-class activities*

- **Map the origins of Nobel Prize winners.** For this activity, each pair or group of students will need a map of the Spanish-speaking world, such as an enlargement of the map in Slide 1.18. Referring to the list of winners in Slide 1.17, students annotate Chile, Colombia, Guatemala, Mexico, Peru, and Spain with the names of their respective Nobel Prize-winning authors, each with the year of their prize and also their literary genre (*poesía, drama, novela,* etc.), which can be determined from the

"Recomendaciones" in Slide 1.17. They may also include a photograph of each writer, which can be found via the URLs listed in Slide 1.19. In that case it will be preferable for students to create their annotated maps electronically rather than resorting to scissors and glue sticks.

- **Pick a favorite Nobel Prize winner.** The teacher distributes copies of the table in Slide 1.17, which includes the official Nobel commendations of the eleven Spanish-speaking winners of the Nobel Prize in Literature. In groups, students read these "Recomendaciones" and on the basis of this information, decide which writer's work they would most want to read. Each group presents and defends its decision.

### Take-home project

- **Profile a Nobel Prize winner.** Each student chooses or is assigned a Hispanic winner of the Nobel Prize in Literature to profile (Slide 1.17). If there are more students than Nobel Prize winners, pairs or groups of students can work together. The profile should include the information shown in Slide 1.20. It can be in the form of a poster, slide presentation, or oral report that can be shared with the class.

## Language features

### The inverted ¿ and ¡ marks

#### Just the facts

The inverted question and exclamation marks (¿ and ¡) are a unique feature of written Spanish. They were formerly used in Galician and Catalan, the two major Romance minority languages of Spain. However, the inverted marks are now optional in Galician, and Catalan's own language academy (the Institut d'Estudis Catalans) officially ruled against them in 1993. The marks serve as an aid to readers, signaling the beginning of a question or exclamation in written Spanish just as a change in tone does in spoken Spanish.

The inverted marks were invented in 1754 by the Real Academia Española (Slide 1.21; the animation adds highlighting for an in-class activity described below). Thirteen years earlier, the Academia had recommended that the regular question and exclamation marks be used both at the beginning and end of questions and exclamations, as per the highlighted text in Slide 1.22; obviously, this first proposal was unsuccessful.

#### Teacher talk

"Los signos invertidos son una invención española. Se inventaron en el año 1754. El español es el único idioma moderno que requiere el uso de los signos invertidos."

*In-class activities*

- **A design project for the inverted marks.** Celebrate the ¿ and ¡ marks with a design project. Students can make large, decorated versions of the marks using a variety of materials. Or the class can make a row of ¿'s and ¡'s that incorporate headshots of the students as the dots. These could be the basis for an "all about me" type of spoken activity.
- **Explore the history of the inverted marks.** As a class, read the selections from the Real Academia Española's original (1754) proposal of the inverted marks (Slide 1.21), and its earlier (1741) proposal for using regular *?* and *!* marks on either side of questions and exclamations (Slide 1.22). Class discussion can center on the three questions in Slide 1.23. The teacher can click on Slide 1.21 to highlight in yellow and blue the portions relevant to the first two questions, respectively (Slide 1.22 is already highlighted).
- **Debate the inverted marks.** Hold an in-class debate on the merits of keeping the ¿ and ¡ marks in Spanish and/or adopting them in English. Slide 1.24 presents some "pro" and "con" arguments.

*Take-home project*

- **Argue for or against the inverted marks.** In essays, PowerPoints, or another medium, students argue for or against keeping the marks in Spanish and/or adopting them in English.

## The eñe

*Just the facts*

Like the inverted ¡ and ¿ marks, the *eñe* is a Spanish creation. Unlike those punctuation marks, it has spread to some degree beyond Spanish. Most languages that use the *eñe*, such as Filipino and Quechua, have cultural connections with Spanish, although some, such as Mandinka and Crimean Tatar, do not. In Portuguese, the tilde (~) designates nasalized vowels.

The letter ñ was originally a shorthand for the double *nn* of Latin words like *annus* 'year,' which was pronounced as a long *n*. The tilde resembles a stylized *n*, and in Old Spanish it was used to abbreviate not just *nn* but *n* in general, to speed up writing and save paper. Examples of this usage, such as *cõ* for *con*, *sõ* for *son*, and *bãcos* for *bancos*, can be seen in Christopher Columbus's letter about his first voyage (Slide 1.25).

As the written Latin *nn* evolved into the Spanish ñ, its sound changed from a long *n* to the modern Spanish ñ sound. Besides *año*, from Latin *annus*, other examples of this change are *niño* (from *ninnus*), *gruñir* (from *grunnire*), and *piña* from *pinna* (originally meaning 'pine cone' and later extended to 'pineapple'). Once the letter ñ was established, it naturally came to also be used for instances of the *ñ* sound that had other origins, such as the *ñ* in *España* (from Latin *Hispania*) and *leña* (from *ligna*). It is one of the least frequently used Spanish letters, ahead of only *x* and the non-native *k* and *w*.

Despite its use in other languages, and its relative rarity in Spanish, the *eñe* has emerged as an iconic symbol of the Spanish language, with the letter or just the tilde appearing frequently in logos and even works of art, as in the examples in Slides 1.26 and 1.27. A 1991 attempt to permit keyboards without out a dedicated *ñ* key to be sold in Spain produced a furor, with protests by Spain's Foreign Ministry, the Real Academia Española, and even the writer Gabriel García Márquez (Slide 1.28, from García Márquez 1991).

*Teacher talk*

"La *eñe* es una invención española aunque se usa también en algunos otros idiomas. La *eñe* fue originalmente una abreviatura de la doble *ene*. Se parece a una *ene* estilizada. [A hand gesture tracing the ~ shape will help.] La *eñe* se ha convertido en el símbolo más reconocido del español. Se usa en logotipos y aun obras de arte."

*In-class activities*

- **Make *eñe* word clouds.** In preparation for this activity, students should identify several words that contain the *eñe* by looking through dictionaries or vocabulary lists. Alternatively, the list in Slide 1.29 (or Slide 1.30, which glosses non-basic vocabulary) can be used to jump-start the activity. In any case students then arrange their selection into a "word cloud," either by hand or using software readily available online, such as wordclouds.com or wordle.net. Another possibility is to align the list of words so that the *eñes* form a column. This can be done by hand or with a word processor.
- **Explore the history of the *eñe*.** The teacher can present the extract from Christopher Columbus's letter about his first voyage to the New World (Slide 1.25) to illustrate the origin of the tilde as an abbreviation for *n*. An alternative is to present the Columbus extract without the tildes identified and ask students to find them (Slide 1.31). A transcription of the text in this extract (without tildes) is in Slide 1.32; a click highlights the words in question.

  Once students understand the origin of the tilde as an abbreviation, the use of *ñ* as shorthand for Latin *nn* will be obvious. While *año* is the best-known example of this development, in a school context it may be safer to avoid the Latin word *annus* and stick to examples such as *niño* and *piña* (see "Just the facts").
- **Discuss the tilde in logos.** Before doing this activity, the teacher will need to follow the links in Slide 1.26 to download copies of various corporate

and institutional logos onto a PowerPoint slide. The class can then discuss the logos. Why did these companies choose to incorporate the tilde? What are the different ways they do this? How do some of them break the rules of Spanish spelling? Are they effective? The take-home project "Exploring the tilde in logos and art" is a more student-centered alternative.

- **Discuss the *eñe* as art.** The class views and discusses José Carlos Martinat's painting *Ñ* (Slide 1.27). Why did this Peruvian artist choose the *eñe* as the subject of the painting? What does this choice say about Hispanic linguistic and cultural identity? Other aspects of the painting to discuss are its large size, unusual materials (including graffiti), and colors, which suggest the Spanish flag. Again, the take-home project "Exploring the tilde in logos and art" is a more student-centered alternative.
- **Gabriel García Márquez defends the *eñe*.** The teacher displays and/or distributes García Márquez's defense of the *eñe* in Spain's *El País* newspaper (Slide 1.28) and explains its context (see "Just the facts"). A class discussion can focus on García Márquez's arguments in defense of the *eñe*. Also, why did a Colombian writer weigh in on a European trade dispute?

## Take-home projects

- **Create a class logo.** Each student (or student group) designs a class logo that incorporates the *eñe*, or just the tilde, and presents it to the class. The class can vote on the best logo.
- **Trace *eñe* etymologies.** Since relatively few words contain an *eñe*, they are a natural basis for a small etymology project. Students divide up the list in Slide 1.29 or 1.30 (omitting the words used as examples in Slide 1.33) and look up their assigned words' etymologies on rae.es, the website of the Real Academia Española. The goal is for students to place their words in a table like the one in Slide 1.33, which has a column for each of the three *eñe* origins mentioned in "Just the facts," plus one for borrowed words. This can be done in three steps: a first pass at home, some class time devoted to helping students resolve any difficulties they encountered (such as obscure abbreviations on the website), and a final pass at home.
- **Explore the tilde in logos and art.** Instead of the teacher accessing the logos and artwork in Slides 1.26 and 1.27, each student (or pair of students) looks up one of these images and presents it to the class. Their presentation should address the questions raised in the in-class activities "The tilde in logos" and "The *eñe* as art." Student pairs could also prepare and present relevant dialogues, such as a conversation between a tilde-loving logo designer and a skeptical CEO, or between the artist José Carlos Martinat and a skeptical art critic.

## The th sound

*Just the facts*

Speakers of English may take for granted the *th* sound of Castilian Spanish *cerveza*, since they use the same sound in English words like *thing*. However, only a small minority of languages have this sound: between four and seven percent (Maddieson 2013). Now that *ll* has merged with *y* in most of the Spanish-speaking world (see Chapter 4), *th* is the only unusual sound remaining in Spanish. Linguists like Maddieson believe that the *th* sound is rare because it is relatively quiet and low-pitched, compared to the much more common *s* sound. This makes it harder to hear and therefore more likely to be lost as a language evolves.

The *th* sound is not generally found in Andalusian (Southern) Spanish, nor in Latin America. These dialects did not lose the *th* sound; rather, the *th* emerged only in Castile, as a relative late (sixteenth century) development; see "The sound changes that shaped Spanish words" in Chapter 3.

For more on the *th* sound, see "Spanish dialects" and "*Yeísmo, seseo*, and *ceceo*," both in Chapter 4.

*Teacher talk*

"El inglés usa el sonido *th*. El español lo usa también, al menos en partes de España. Pero se usa en pocos otros idiomas. Es el único sonido inusual del español."

*In-class activity*

• **Hear the *th*.** Spanish students in the United States are not normally exposed to the Castilian *th* unless their teacher happens to be from that region or has adopted that pronunciation. To make up this deficit, and thus increase students' awareness of the *th* sound, the class can listen to native speaker pronunciations recorded on the crowdsourced Forvo.com website. In preparation for this activity, the instructor (or students; see below) searches Forvo.com for words containing the *th* sound, such as *cerveza* and *cien* (Slide 1.34), and identifies individual pronunciations contributed by Spaniards that are clear examples of the *th*. Words that combine an *s* and a *th*, such as *social* and *cesar*, also make for good listening.

   Forvo can also be used to play different speakers' pronunciations of a single word, such as *cero*. Can students pick out the Castilian pronunciations?

*Take-home project*

• **Find *th* examples.** In this project students do the groundwork for the in-class activity "Hear the *th*" by finding clear examples of *th* words (such as those on Slide 1.34) on Forvo.com. Teachers could require students to find only a clear *th* pronunciation of 'their' word, or both a *th* and an *s* example, if available. Students should submit their examples, each identified by URL and speaker name, in time for the teacher to review them before playing them in class.

### The mega-preposition en

#### Just the facts

The Spanish preposition *en* covers a broader range of meanings than its English translation *in* – and, for that matter, its equivalent in most other languages. In particular, *en* (and likewise Portuguese *em*) encompasses the concepts of both 'in' and 'on,' so that the *café* is *en la taza* ('in') and the *taza* is *en la mesa* ('on'). This combination of meanings is highly unusual. Most languages have separate terms for 'in' and 'on,' although not all make the exact division found in English (Bowerman and Choi 2001). For good measure, *en* also corresponds to some uses of English *at*.

#### Teacher talk

"La preposición española *en* es una 'superpreposición', una preposición con una amplia variedad de significados. Solo el español y el portugués usan la misma palabra para 'in' y 'on'."

#### In-class activity

- **Highlight the range of *en*.** Students create an art project to highlight the difference between the Spanish and English prepositions. Each student chooses three uses of *en* from Slide 1.35, one each corresponding to the meanings 'in,' 'on,' and 'at,' illustrates them, and labels them in Spanish and in English. It is particularly pleasing to pick three uses that can be combined in a single illustration, e.g. *una cuchara en la taza en la mesa en la playa* 'a spoon IN the cup ON the table AT the beach.'

### The two imperfect subjunctives

#### Just the facts

The Spanish imperfect subjunctive can be formed either with -*ra* endings, as in *estuviera* or *hiciéramos*, or with -*se* endings, as in *estuviese* or *hiciésemos*. The -*se* subjunctive dates back to Old Spanish, while the -*ra* subjunctive is a Siglo de Oro innovation. (The original Latin imperfect subjunctive was lost, as described in Chapter 3.) Today the -*ra* forms are in general more frequent than the -*se* forms. However, both are understood throughout the

Spanish-speaking world, and are still used actively in written Spanish and even in conversation, depending on dialect.

The continued existence of two parallel forms for a grammatical structure is extremely unusual, or even unique. Typically such duplication is found only for individual words or small groups of words, such as English *dove/dived* or French *je m'assieds/assois* 'I sit down' and *je rassieds/ rassois* for 'I replace.' In contrast, the *-ra/-se* difference applies to every Spanish verb.

Expressions such as *Fuera lo que fuese* 'no matter what' exploit the duplicate forms, as can Spanish literature; see examples in Slides 1.36 and 1.37.

*Teacher talk*

"Es sorprendente que el español tenga dos versiones del imperfecto del subjuntivo. Es el único ejemplo conocido de tales formas gemelas en la gramática de cualquier idioma. El contraste entre las dos versiones del imperfecto del subjuntivo se explota en el refrán *fuera lo que fuese* y de vez en cuando en la literatura también."

*In-class activity*

• **Exploit the *-ra/-se* contrast.** The teacher explains the expression *fuera lo que fuese* and has students interpret the similar turns of phrase in Slide 1.36. Students then have the opportunity to invent their own uses of this structure. Some examples might be *Estudiara que estudiase, los exámenes son difíciles para mí* or *Trabajara que trabajase, nunca tiene bastante dinero*. Students can also discuss how the authors of the examples in Slide 1.37 exploit the *-ra/-se* contrast. What would these sentences lose if the authors had only used one of the subjunctive alternatives?

*Take-home project*

• **Trace the takeover of the *-ra* subjunctive.** Google Books's Ngram Viewer tracks the frequency, over time, of words in all the books Google has digitized (http://books.google.com/ngrams; Michel et al. 2011). This tool is an easy and even fun way to see how the *-ra* imperfect subjunctive has displaced the *-se* subjunctive in the past several decades. As an example, Slide 1.38 shows the changing frequencies of *tuviera* and *tuviese* between the years 1800 and 2000, with *tuviera* (in blue) overtaking *tuviese* (in red) around 1890. Each student can create a corresponding graph for a different verb by typing the two verb forms into the search bar, separated by a comma, and selecting "Spanish" for the corpus. Students can print the graphs and bring them to class for comparison, or share them electronically.

### The variety of Spanish past tenses

*Just the facts*

Spanish has many ways to talk about the past, including the preterite, imperfect, present perfect, pluperfect, past progressive, and *acabar de* (Slide 1.39). In a classic cross-linguistic survey of verb systems, Dahl (1985, 171) found that all six of these Spanish past tenses met the criteria for "major Tense/Mood/Aspect (TMA)" categories because they were frequent and could appear in affirmative, active main clauses. (These criteria ruled out, for example, the Spanish imperfect subjunctive.) Of the sixty-three other languages Dahl surveyed, only Catalan and Kikuyu, a Bantu language of Africa with seven major TMA categories, surpassed Spanish. This means that Spanish has a richer past tense repertoire than the other Romance languages and English as well as Arabic, Japanese, German, Greek, Russian, Mandarin, Hungarian, and dozens of other languages Dahl surveyed.

As discussed in the Introduction, every chapter of this book addresses some aspect of the Spanish past tense. See "Preterite and imperfect" in Chapter 2, "The evolution of the Spanish verb system" and "The extreme irregularity of *ir* and *ser*" in Chapter 3, "Non-standard verb forms" and "Variation in verb use" in Chapter 4, and "Order of acquisition of verb tenses" in Chapter 5.

*Teacher talk*

"Hay seis maneras principales de expresar el pasado en español. Esto es más que tiene la gran mayoría de otros idiomas."

*In-class activities*

- **Use the major past tenses.** Working alone or in pairs, students write a paragraph that attempts to incorporate all six of Dahl's major past tenses for Spanish (Slide 1.39). This paragraph could summarize a recent news event, a reading, or a short video.
- **Represent the major past tenses.** Spanish teachers sometimes represent the imperfect as a wavy line, to symbolize continuity, and the preterite as a vertical line, to symbolize completion. Working alone or in pairs, students devise a set of symbols that represent each of the six main past tenses. They then explain their symbols to the class.

*Take-home project*

- **Quantify past tense usage.** Because many newspaper articles describe something that has already happened, they are a ready source of texts written in the past tense. In this activity, students analyze past tense usage in different newspaper articles and combine their results to give an overall picture of which expressions of the past tense are most frequent. This activity is most interesting if (i) students predict the likely results ahead of time and (ii) some students analyze news stories from Spain, where the present perfect has been gaining ground vis-à-vis the preterite (Chapter 4), while others focus on Latin America.

To carry out this project, each student chooses a Spanish-language newspaper article that describes an event that has already taken place, such as a soccer game or a government decision. They then record and total the first fifty or so past tense verb forms in the article that were in one the six main forms of the Spanish past tense, as in the top half of Slide 1.40. Students' data summaries can then be combined into a single chart as in the bottom half of the slide. At this point students can compare predicted versus actual usage, and also compare Latin American and peninsular Spanish.

### Gendered first and second person pronouns

*Just the facts*

It may surprise speakers of Spanish and English that most languages do not have separate masculine and feminine pronouns (Siewierska 2013). Just as English makes do with neuter *they*, most languages combine 'he' and 'she' into a single pronoun such as Finnish *hän* and Hindi *vah*. Of languages that do have gendered pronouns, most do so only in the third person singular (as in English), or in both singular and plural third person (as in French *il/elle*, *ils/elles*). Spanish is unusual because it has distinct masculine and feminine pronouns not only in the third person (*él/ella* and *ellos/ellas*), but also in the first person plural (*nosotros/nosotras*) and, in Spain, in the second person plural as well (*vosotros/vosotras*).

This oddity arose relatively late in the Old Spanish period (fourteenth or fifteenth century), when speakers began to add *otros/otras* to Old Spanish *nos* 'we' and *vos* 'you (plural),' which had descended from the identical words in Latin.

Because *nosotras* is both feminine and plural, it can signal female solidarity, somewhat like the expression *Girl Power* in English. This can be seen in titles of books that either profile famous women or exemplify "chick lit," public events, and political slogans (Slides 1.41–1.43). To show the power of *nosotras*, teachers can download images associated with these examples via the links in these slides and share them with the class.

*Teacher talk*

"Es bastante común que un idioma tenga palabras distintas para *él* y *ella*, y también para *ellos* y *ellas*. Pero el español es inusual porque también tiene *nosotros* y *nosotras*, y, en España, *vosotros* y *vosotras*. Pocos idiomas tienen tales pronombres masculinos y femeninos. La palabra *nosotras* en particular puede expresar un significado feminista."

*In-class activities*

The first of these activities has a corresponding take-home project; the others could be done at home instead of in class.

• **Discuss *nosotras*-themed literature, events, or slogans.** This activity requires some set-up time on the part of the instructor (or students: see the corresponding take-home project). The teacher follows the links in Slides 1.41–1.43 to download images of *nosotras*-themed book covers, event posters, and political protests. (The teacher can instead simply use the names of the corresponding books, events, and slogans as shown on the slides, but the corresponding images are more stimulating.) These images then serve as the basis for class discussion. For example, the teacher might ask students to imagine the likely plot of one of the novels, what they might see at a *nosotras*-themed art exhibit, or how they interpret the political slogans. In each case, the class should consider how the word *nosotras* itself communicates the likely intent of the book, event, or protest.

• **Write a poem on the theme of *nosotras* or *vosotras*.** A *nosotras* or *vosotras* poem might focus on two girls or women (perhaps sisters, a mother and daughter, or best friends), on a specific group of girls or women (perhaps friends or female relations), or on girls or women in general. If the teacher requires an acrostic structure, the poems can be combined with a targeted presentation or review of relevant vocabulary and/or grammar. For example, the adjective acrostic in Slide 1.44 uses eight adjectives that begin with *n-o-s-o-t-r-a-s* (Slide 1.45 lists several others), all in the feminine plural, while the *vosotras* verb acrostic in Slide 1.46 exercises the *imperfecto* past tense.

• **Design a *nosotras.com* website.** Students work in pairs or groups to design a possible website entitled *nosotras.com*. Their work should address the design issues listed in Slide 1.47. Teacher beware: the actual *nosotras.com* website, based in Barcelona, includes sexual content as well as fitness, fashion, and so on, while *nosotrasonline.com* is the online presence of *Nosotras*, a brand of sanitary napkins (and itself a telling use of the pronoun).

• **Design a book cover for a *nosotras*-themed book.** Slide 1.41 contains links to several books with feminine or feminist themes that incorporate *nosotras* in their titles. In this activity students or pairs of students create front and back book covers for their own fiction or non-fiction *nosotras*-related book. Besides an imaginative title, the front cover should incorporate appropriate artwork and the back cover should give a suitable blurb.

- **Propose a *nosotras*-based event.** Students propose a *nosotras*-themed cultural or political event. Proposals should include a title, a one-sentence mission statement, a one-paragraph description, and a schedule of activities.

*Take-home projects*

- **Explore *nosotras* in literature, events, or politics.** Instead of the teacher downloading images of the books, events, and slogans in Slides 1.41–1.43, each student (or pair of students) looks up one of these images and presents it to the class. Their presentation should address the questions raised in the in-class activity "Discussing *nosotras*-themed literature, events, or slogans." Student pairs could also prepare and present relevant dialogues, such as a conversation between a writer and her book cover designer.
- **Ask a native speaker about *nosotras*.** How do native speakers view *nosotras*? Are they even aware of it? Do they consciously choose between *nosotros* and *nosotras*, or is it automatic? Do they perceive a feminist nuance to the pronoun? This activity requires students to work with a native speaker partner as described in the Introduction, except that the partner must be female. (If a student already has a partner who is male, the student should pair up with a classmate whose partner is female.) As a preliminary, students could use class time to decide on a common set of questions for the interview.

The following references are cited in this chapter's text and/or its accompanying PowerPoint presentation.

## References

Bowerman, M., and S. Choi. 2001. Shaping meanings for language: Universal and language-specific in the acquisition of spatial semantic categories. In *Language acquisition and conceptual development*, eds. M. Bowerman and S. C. Levinson, 475–511. Cambridge: Cambridge University Press.

Dahl, O. 1985. *Tense and aspect systems.* Oxford: Basil Blackwell.

Dryer, M. S., and M. Haspelmath, eds. 2013. *The world atlas of language structures online.* Leipzig: Max Planck Institute for Evolutionary Anthropology. http://wals.info.

Eberhard, D. M., G. F. Simons, and D. D. Fennig, eds. 2020. *Ethnologue: Languages of the world.* 23rd ed. Dallas, TX: SIL International. Online version: http://www.ethnologue.com.

García Márquez, G. 1991. García Márquez defiende la eñe. *El País,* May 14.

Herreros, E. 2005. *La codorniz de Enrique Herreros.* Madrid: Edaf.

Maddieson, I. 2013. Presence of uncommon consonants. In Dryer and Haspelmath 2013, ch. 19.

Mariló. 2012. Cuentos desde mi rincón: Una segunda oportunidad. *Villanueva de los Castillos y El Almendro: Cuentos desde mi rincón*. August 1. http://mdjigar. blogspot.com/2012/08/cuentos-una-segunda-oportunidad.html.

Martínez, G. 2008. *La muerte lenta de Luciana B.* New York: RAYO.

Michel, J-B., Y. K. Shen, A. P. Aiden, A. Veres, M. K. Gray, The Google Books Team, J. P. Pickett, et al. 2011. Quantitative analysis of culture using millions of digitized books. *Science* 331: 176–82.

*Notimérica*. 2010. Chávez dice que hará caso a la RAE y se llamará "ávez." November 12. https://www.notimerica.com/politica/noticia-venezuela-chavez-dice-hara-caso-rae-llamara-avez-20101112171114.html.

Penny, R. 2002. *A history of the Spanish language*. 2nd ed. Cambridge: Cambridge University Press.

Pérez-Reverte, A. 2000. *La carta esférica*. Mexico City: Santillana.

Real Academia Española (RAE). 1741. *Orthographia española*. Madrid: Real Academia Española. http://www.cervantesvirtual.com/servlet/SirveObras/011596301089204107 60035/index.htm.

———. 1763. *Ortografía de la lengua castellana*. 3rd ed. Madrid: Pérez de Soto. https://archive.org/details/ortografiadelale00madruoft. The section cited is identical to that of the 2nd edition (1754) but is more legible.

———. 2010. *Principales novedades de la última edición de la* Ortografía de la lengua española. https://www.rae.es/sites/default/files/Principales_novedades_de_la_Ortografia_de_la_lengua_espanola.pdf.

Sierra i Fabra, J. 2008. *Cuatro días de enero*. Barcelona: Delbosillo.

Siewierska, A. 2013. Gender distinctions in independent personal pronouns. In Dryer and Haspelmath 2013, ch. 44.

# Chapter 2

# How is Spanish similar to other languages?

In this chapter the focus shifts from elements of Spanish that are unusual or unique, as presented in Chapter 1, to elements that are found in many other languages. It is a relatively short chapter because it concentrates specifically on ways that Spanish is similar to many other languages yet different from English. These include aspects of written Spanish (limited use of capital letters), phonology (e.g. the trilled *r*), and grammar (e.g. grammatical gender). Learning that these features are in fact widespread – and that, in many cases, English is the "odd man out" – can motivate students to accept and master them. The one exception is the greater irregularity of frequent verbs in both Spanish and English. In this case, recognizing this feature as a shared characteristic may provide its own motivation, or at least acceptance.

Later chapters address other aspects of Spanish that it shares with English as well as other languages. For example, the historical upgrade in meaning of *caballo* from 'nag' to 'horse' is similar to that of *bad* and *sick*, now used as compliments in contemporary American slang (Chapter 3). Dialectal variations in Spanish vocabulary, such as *piscina* versus *alberca*, are analogous to English differences like *lift* versus *elevator* (Chapter 4). And children's verb conjugation errors, such as *\*abrido* for *abierto*, parallel infantile errors in English such as *\*falled* for *fell* (Chapter 5).

This chapter includes a wide range of activities to bring its topics to life. Some of these **celebrate** these features of Spanish: for example, writing sentences that push the boundaries of the personal *a*. Others encourage students to **explore** them: for example, relating verb frequency and irregularity. Some delve into **history**: for example, tracing the development of the Spanish second person pronouns. Others provide opportunities for students to **engage** with these features; for example, dedicating a set amount of time per day to mastering the trilled *r*. Finally, some **compare** Spanish to other languages that share the features; for example, comparing the genders of a set of words in Spanish and another language. For a full list of the chapter's activities and projects, and their suitability for different levels of instruction, see Appendices A and B.

## Limited capitalization

### Just the facts

Spanish only capitalizes proper nouns, first words in sentences and titles of works, and abbreviated personal titles (Slide 2.1). Almost all other languages that use the Roman alphabet limit capitalization in the same way. The only exceptions are English, which capitalizes days of the week, months of the year, and certain other word types, and German, which capitalizes all nouns (see again Slide 2.1).

### Teacher talk

"Casi todos los idiomas que usan el alfabeto romano tienen el mismo uso de mayúsculas que el español. El inglés y el alemán son las únicas excepciones."

### In-class activity

- **Highlight Spanish/English capitalization differences.** Individually or in pairs, students compete to write a Spanish paragraph that uses as many words as possible that are not capitalized in Spanish but would be in English. Students should use a variety of the word types shown in Slide 2.1, but they should not use lists of words (e.g. *católicos, musulmanes y judíos*), nor specific words that appear in the slide.

## Five vowels

### Just the facts

Spanish has five vowel sounds, represented by the five vowel letters *a, e, i, o,* and *u*. Worldwide, five-vowel systems are the most common, and typically resemble that of Spanish (Slide 2.2, based on Schwartz et al. 1997). The English vowel system, which uses the same five letters to represent twelve vowel sounds (Slide 2.3), is an outlier.

### Teacher talk

"El español tiene cinco letras vocálicas, y cinco sonidos vocálicos básicos: *a, e, i, o, u*. En los idiomas del mundo, es más común tener cinco vocales, y con mayor frecuencia, estas son las cinco vocales del español."

### In-class activities

- **Compare Spanish and English vowels.** Working in pairs, students compare the twelve vowels of English with the five vowels of Spanish (Slide 2.3).

Which five English vowels are most similar to the five Spanish vowels, and which are not present in Spanish? (Clicking on the slide reveals the answer.) As a follow-up, the class can discuss how this vowel mismatch challenges native English students when they learn Spanish, and vice versa. Which adjustment is likely to be more difficult?

- **Articulate the Spanish vowel triangle.** The Spanish *aeiou* vowel set is common across languages because it makes optimal use of the space available in the mouth. Slides 2.4 and 2.5 show how the tongue rises high in the mouth to produce the vowels *i* and *u*, and drops down for the *a*; *e* and *o* are in between. (The first slide is a schematic, while the second shows actual MRIs of a Spanish speaker (Gurlekian, Elisei, and Elita 2004).) Likewise, the tongue pushes toward the front of the mouth to produce *i* and *e*, and pulls back for *u* and *o*; *a* is in between. To feel these differences for themselves, students can compare their tongue positions in the words *ti* versus *tú* (front vs. back), *y* versus *a* (high vs. low), and *u* versus *a* (again, high vs. low). They can also feel the tongue moving down-and-up and front-to-back as they move through the sequence *i-e-a-o-u*. (The jaw and lips move as well, but these movements are secondary.)
- **Analyze *palabras panvocálicas*.** A charming consequence of the compact vowel system of Spanish is that one can identify many words in which all five vowels appear exactly once, such as *murciélago*. Slide 2.6 shows seventy-five of these *palabras panvocálicas*. Because these words are long, they tend to be outside of everyday vocabulary, and so afford an opportunity for vocabulary enrichment; many have English cognates. An in-class discussion can revolve around topics such as false cognates, compounds, suffixes, prefixes, and Greek roots; see Slide 2.7 for examples.

*Take-home project*

- **Write a story with *palabras panvocálicas*.** As an at-home follow-up to the in-class activity described above, students write a story using as many words as possible from the list in Slide 2.6 or from the full list at juegosdepalabras (2020). The more original the story, and the more *palabras panvocálicas* it uses, the better. Teachers may require students to include some number of words that they did not know before in addition to familiar vocabulary and cognates.

### Simple syllables

*Just the facts*

Spanish syllables are mostly short and simple (see Slide 2.8). They normally consist of a vowel or vowel sequence either on its own, paired with a single consonant, or sandwiched between two consonants. A more complex syllable can begin and/or end with two consonants, but only a few consonant sequences are possible.

A majority of languages worldwide follow the Spanish pattern, allowing only certain types of complex syllables (Slide 2.9, based on Maddieson 2013). Some languages disallow complex syllables entirely: Hawaiian, for example, allows, at most, a single consonant followed by one or two vowels. At the other extreme, English allows consonant combinations that are longer than those of Spanish, as in *strengths*, or that are short but disallowed in Spanish, as in *dwarf*.

A knowledge of syllable structure can be of practical value when writing without a word processor since hyphenation is allowed only at syllable boundaries. It is also crucial when speaking a *jerigonza* (Spanish "Pig Latin"), as described in Chapter 5. Syllable structure rules also shed light on two interesting aspects of Spanish words. First, the *e-* that Spanish has added to the beginning of many words serves the purpose of breaking up disallowed consonant sequences; for example, Latin *spatha* 'sword' emerged in Spanish as *es.pa.da*, and English *stress* was borrowed as *es.trés*. Second, the syllable structure rules contribute to the greater length of Spanish words, compared to English, because English allows a greater variety of syllables. Likewise, Hawaiian words are longer than Spanish words. (The fact that English has more sounds than Spanish, especially vowels, and Hawaiian fewer, also contributes to these differences.)

## Teacher talk

"Las sílabas españolas son bastante básicas, como *a, tú, cuan.do,* o *es.tán.* Se permiten unas sílabas más complejas, por ejemplo *tres* o *vals*, pero con restricciones. Este tipo de sistema – sílabas mayormente básicas y unas complejas – es el más típico en los idiomas del mundo."

## In-class activities

* **Tally syllable types.** This activity heightens students' awareness of the five types of Spanish syllables, as defined in Slide 2.8. Each student works with the same short text, dividing each word into syllables and then tallying, for each word and in total, the number of syllables of each type in the text. The example in Slide 2.10 analyzes the first line of Pablo Neruda's "Poema XX."

  To make this activity more challenging, the instructor can choose a text that includes a variety of vowel sequences. Some sequences form single syllables and others divide into two (compare *seis* and *ve.o*), following the rules summarized in Slide 2.11.

* **Compare Spanish and English word lengths.** This activity relates the syllable structure rules of Spanish to its relatively long words. For a given set of vocabulary, such as clothing terms, students compare the number

of syllables in the Spanish words and their English equivalents. Furthermore, they identify the English words that contain a syllable type not allowed in Spanish. Slide 2.12 shows an example.

Note that the presence of a non-Spanish syllable type in a specific English word does not automatically make it longer than its Spanish equivalent; rather, the point of the activity is to highlight the general relationship between syllable structure and word length in the two languages.

### The trilled r

*Just the facts*

The trilled *r* is a stumbling block for many Spanish language learners. English speakers generally master the flapped (or tapped) *r* of words like *pero* without much difficulty, since it resembles the English intervocalic *d* in words like *butter*. But the trill is completely alien to English, so that students who did not acquire it on their own as young children, perhaps to imitate the sound of a motor, often struggle to learn it later in life.

This difficulty belies the fact that trilled *r*'s like the Spanish *r* are the most common type of *r* sound found across languages. They account for almost half of the *r* sounds analyzed in one comprehensive study, with flaps or taps as in *pero* in second place (Slide 2.13, based on Maddieson 2009). In contrast, the gliding English *r* is quite unusual. The back-of-the-mouth trill of German and French fall into the substantial "other" category.

See Chapter 4 for dialectal variation in the Spanish *r*, and Chapter 5 for its first-language acquisition.

*Teacher talk*

"En los idiomas del mundo hay muchas maneras de pronunciar la *r*, pero la pronunciación *erre* española es la más común. La *r* del inglés es mucho menos común."

*In-class activity*

• **Hear the trilled *r* in other languages.** To illustrate the normality of the Spanish *r*, instructors can play recordings of words with the same sound in other languages. Slide 2.14 provides links to such words on the crowdsourced Forvo.com website. Teachers should listen to different speakers' pronunciations in advance to identify those with a clear trill. Teachers may wish to tell students ahead of time what languages they will be hearing and ask them to try to identify each word's source language.

*Take-home project*

- **Tackle the trilled *r*.** This activity challenges students to devote an agreed-upon amount of time, perhaps five minutes twice a day for two weeks, to improving their pronunciation of the trilled *r*, and to document their progress. As a first step, each student (or pair of students) should pick a learning technique (or techniques) to adopt. An Internet search will suggest several different techniques, including written and/or video instructions. Students should pick their favorite technique(s) and justify their choice. During the practice period, students should document their progress in a written or video journal. Those who can already pronounce the *r* can serve as mentors or coaches in this process and should document that experience as well.

## Special locative

*Just the facts*

The contrast between *ser* and *estar* challenges native English speakers because both Spanish verbs translate as 'to be.' A simple historical perspective can help to elucidate the contrast: *estar* comes from the Latin verb *stare* 'to stand' and thus originated as a locative, i.e. a word used to express location. This remains one of the primary functions of *estar*, and the verb's many other uses, such as describing temporary states, evolved from that core use.

It is worth noting, for the sake of completeness, that *ser* also originated in part as a locative. Many forms of the verb, including the infinitive *ser* and the present subjunctive, come from the Latin verb *sedere* 'to sit' instead of *esse* 'to be' (see "The extreme irregularity of *ser* and *ir*" in Chapter 3). However, these forms have since lost their locative flavor; *ser* only expresses location in modern Spanish when describing an event (e.g. *La fiesta es en la casa de Jimena*). This oddity confounds children learning Spanish as a first language as well as Spanish students (Chapter 5).

The contrast embodied in *ser/estar* is not unusual: more than two-thirds of languages worldwide have a special locative (see Slide 2.15, based on Stassen 2013). Like Spanish, many of these languages have two verbs meaning 'to be.' However, in some languages the locative is not a verb, but another word type such as a preposition. In still other languages the locative is a verb, and other uses of 'be' are implied rather than explicitly expressed – a kind of *Me Tarzan, you Jane* approach. Slide 2.16 illustrates these different types of locative/non-locative contrasts.

*Teacher talk*

"*Estar* es nuestro verbo especial para expresar la ubicación ('location'). Muchos otros idiomas también tienen una manera especial de expresar la ubicación. No tienen un verbo 'to be' general, como tiene el inglés."

*Take-home project*

- **WebQuest: Explore the history of *estar*.** In this WebQuest, students research the history of the verb *estar*. Questions for the WebQuest are in Slide 2.17; successive clicks will reveal the answers successively, as well as follow-up questions for in-class discussion.

## Multiple 'you' pronouns

*Just the facts*

Spanish-speaking countries use a variety of different pronouns to mean 'you.' But all differentiate in some way between singular and plural, and likewise between informal and formal. These Spanish pronouns can challenge English-speaking students because standard modern English only has a single 'you' pronoun. It may be helpful to remind students of the archaic English *thou*, which once expressed intimacy (like *tú*), and of the *y'all* plural pronoun of the American South.

As shown in Slide 2.18, English is clearly exceptional in having only a single word for 'you.' Most dramatically, ninety-six percent of languages distinguish between singular and plural 'you' (Ingram 1978). In fact, forty-two percent take this distinction farther, using a special 'you' pronoun to address only two people. In addition, more than twenty-five percent of languages have a formal/informal distinction, as in Spanish; this includes many languages with multiple levels of formality (Helmbrecht 2013). The formal/informal distinction is especially common in Europe (Slide 2.19), meaning that Spanish was under some "peer pressure" to develop and maintain such a distinction.

For dialectal differences in Spanish pronoun usage, see Chapter 4.

*Teacher talk*

"El inglés solo tiene un pronombre 'you' mientras el español tiene varios. A este respecto el español es normal y el inglés es inusual. La gran mayoría de idiomas tienen un contraste entre 'you' singular y plural, y muchos idiomas, sobre todo en Europa, tienen un contraste entre 'you' informal y formal."

*In-class activities*

- **Trace the development of the Spanish 'you' pronouns.** Slide 2.20 summarizes the development of these pronouns from Latin to modern Spanish. Working in pairs, students identify and write down the main change(s) between each historical stage in the language, based on the slide. They then compare their findings as a class, and discuss why the changes may have taken place. Slides 2.21–2.23 supply some answers from a linguistic perspective, including parallel phenomena from other languages.

- **Argue for or against multiple 'you' pronouns.** Working in small teams, students discuss the advantages and disadvantages of Spanish's multiple 'you' pronouns. For example, the use of singular versus plural pronouns can avoid ambiguity (an advantage), but using the wrong pronoun (informal or formal) may cause offense (a disadvantage). Each group then shares its conclusion(s) and reasoning with the class. The class may go on to carry out a debate between teams that favor or disfavor the multiple pronouns. Teams may pick their own side for the debate or the teacher can assign the sides.
- **Choose *tú* or *usted* in a business context.** Working in small teams, students invent a business; teachers can accelerate this step by listing possible business ideas to choose from (some are in Slide 2.24) or assigning a business to each team. Each team then discusses whether their business's website should address its customers as *tú*, *usted*, or a combination. Students can read Tomasena (2020), a brief guide on the subject, at the beginning of the activity or as preparatory homework, and use its principles to guide their discussion. Afterward, they present to the class their business idea, their choice of pronoun(s), and the reasoning behind their choice.
- **Wear a tie to practice *tú* and *usted*.** As suggested by Rusch, Domínguez, and Caycedo Garner (2007, 4), a teacher can randomly distribute neckties to some students in the class before doing any speaking activity. These students must then be addressed as *usted* during the activity. To save time, students can simply drape the ties around their necks or tie them like a scarf.

### Take-home project

- **Ask a native speaker about their pronoun usage.** This activity requires students to work with a native speaker partner as described in the Introduction. It is an ideal topic for such an activity because most Hispanics are highly attuned to the different second person pronouns. As a preliminary, students could use class time to decide on a common set of questions for the interview, such as those in Slide 2.25. Students can summarize their findings in a written, oral, or graphic report.

### Frequent irregular verbs

### Just the facts

Irregular Spanish verbs are doubly problematic for students because they are not only numerous, but also frequent (Slide 2.26). This is not a coincidence, but rather a common feature across languages. Irregularities in infrequent verbs tend to get "ironed out" or "corrected" over time, whereas frequent irregulars have more staying power simply because speakers say and hear them more often. The most frequent verbs in English are irregular as well (same slide).

See also "The extreme irregularity of *ser* and *ir*" in Chapter 3.

### Teacher talk

"Los verbos más frecuentes del español son irregulares. Esto es común en otros idiomas también, incluso el inglés, porque los verbos irregulares que no se usan mucho no mantienen su irregularidad."

### In-class activities

- **Link frequency and irregularity.** This activity encourages students to discover the linkage between verb frequency and irregularity for themselves. Instead of Slide 2.26 the teacher should show Slide 2.27, which lists the twenty-four most frequent Spanish verbs. When students identify the irregular verbs on this list, they will see that they cluster toward the beginning of the list, i.e. the most frequent verbs. Slide 2.26 can then be shown to highlight the similarity between Spanish and English in this regard.
- **Think about irregular verbs.** As a follow-up to the previous activity, the class can discuss whether the verbs *llegar*, *creer*, and *parecer* (Slide 2.27), as well as related verbs, are truly irregular. *Llegar* and *creer* have spelling changes in certain forms that reflect, rather than alter, these forms' expected pronunciations. Do these spelling changes alone make the verbs "irregular?" *Parecer* is a "-zco" verb, like almost all verbs whose infinitives end in *-ecer* and also *-acer*, *-ocer*, and *-ucir* (e.g. *nacer*, *conocer*, and *deducir*). Should these verbs be considered a subclass of Spanish verbs with a predictable conjugation, rather than actually irregular?

### Preterite and imperfect

### Just the facts

Mastering the difference between the preterite and imperfect past tenses is probably the single greatest intellectual challenge for an English-speaking Spanish student. These two expressions of the past focus treat past occurrences as either complete or continuous, respectively. Almost half of languages around the world encode this distinction in their grammars (Slide 2.28, Dahl and Velupillai 2013). English does not; for example, it uses the same verb form in *Yesterday I ate dinner at 6:30* and *When I was a girl I always ate dinner with my parents*, in this case relying on the adverb *always* to capture the aspectual nuance. English does have a progressive past tense (*was eating*) that overlaps with some uses of the imperfect. However, the essential point here is that basic past tense forms like *ate* can be either "perfective" or "imperfective"; see Penny (2002, 164) for a succinct explanation of these various aspects of the past tense. A further challenge is that the preterite and imperfect are only two of six principal ways to express the past in Spanish, an unusual feature of the language discussed in Chapter 1.

The distinction between completed and continuing events is simple in the abstract but elusive in practice. For this reason, many teachers train their students to rely on various rules of thumb when deciding between preterite and imperfect. Some of these rules concern the type of past occurrence; for example, students may learn to use the preterite to describe beginnings and endings (e.g. *empezó* and *terminó*) and the imperfect to describe the weather (e.g. *llovía*). Other rules focus on contextual clues, such as specific time frames for the preterite (e.g. *todo el día*) and *mientras* for the imperfect. While helpful, the former rules are fallible (e.g. *El orador empezaba a hablar cuando el micrófono falló; Ayer llovió durante tres horas*) and the latter are often absent in actual speech or writing. Sooner or later students have to grapple with the aspectual difference itself.

The visual metaphors in Slides 2.29 and 2.30 can help. Slide 2.29 depicts the preterite as a closed box containing a past occurrence (in this case the life of El Cid), and the imperfect as an open box that "unpacks" the occurrence, telling us more about it. This metaphor is particularly helpful when deciding between *fue* and *era*. Slide 2.30 depicts multiple preterite events as discrete and sequenceable, like beads on a string. This metaphor is particularly useful when teaching students to construct narratives. The animation in Slide 2.30 shows how one can use the imperfect to add color to a bare-bones preterite narrative, an exercise described later in this section. Students may be interested in learning that children usually acquire the two tenses in this same order, i.e. preterite before imperfect (Slide 5.19).

Regardless of the approach a teacher takes, it is likely that students will have to engage with the preterite/imperfect distinction multiple times as they continue to study Spanish, with each pass moving them closer to mastery.

### Teacher talk

"La diferencia entre el pretérito y el imperfecto tiene que ver con nuestra perspectiva hacia un evento pasado. ¿Lo vemos como un episodio único y completo, o uno cuyo comienzo y fin ignoramos? Esta diferencia, que se encuentra en muchos idiomas alrededor del mundo, llega a ser más clara con práctica."

### In-class activity

*   **Write preterite/imperfect narratives.** In this activity students, individually or in pairs, recreate the three steps shown in Slide 2.30 for combining

the preterite and imperfect in narratives. The first step is to write the bare bones of a narrative using the preterite. A series of four events is adequate: what happened first? next? next-to-last? last? The next two steps add "color commentary," a useful term from sports journalism. As shown with a first click, students can add details about the events. (This is like "opening the box" in the previous slide.) As shown with a second click, students can also add two types of background information: overall background, of the "used to" or nostalgic variety, and background specific to an individual event, normally prefaced with *mientras* (or *cuando*). An optional final click adds the helpful English phrases "used to" and "while."

It is important for students to share their work throughout this exercise so that the teacher (or fellow students) can critique it. As a final step, students should rewrite their narratives formatted as normal prose. As a follow-up activity they can exchange papers and label the different parts of their classmates' narratives.

### Take-home project

- **Test preterite/imperfect guidelines.** Many Spanish textbooks and teachers offer "rules of thumb," as described above, for when to use the preterite versus the imperfect. Google's Ngram Viewer provides an easy way to test these guidelines against Google's large corpus of Spanish text (http://books.google.com/ngrams, Michel et al. 2011). Students can test comparisons such as *hizo/hacía calor* (one expects more examples of *hacía*), *estuvieron/estaban tristes* (*estaban*), *empezamos/empezábamos* (*empezamos*), and *terminaron/terminaban* (*terminaron*). Slide 2.31 shows *empezamos* versus *empezábamos* as a sample graph, with *empezamos* in the lead for the last two centuries.

  In preparation for this project, the class should brainstorm a list of comparisons to be done at home, based on what they know about the use of these tenses. Whenever possible, students should avoid first and third person singular verb forms because the imperfect forms are ambiguous; for example, *leía* corresponds to both *leí* and *leyó*. (Hence the inclusion of *calor* in the *hizo/hacía* comparison.)

## Gender

### Just the facts

Grammatical gender is ubiquitous in Spanish: most nouns are either masculine or feminine, and adjectives, articles, and pronouns must all agree with their head noun. In contrast, English retains only traces of grammatical gender, such as the pronouns *he* and *she*, and a few gendered objects such as ships, which are conventionally female. As shown in Slide 2.32 (based on Corbett 2013a), almost half of languages worldwide have gender agreement systems, many with more than two gender categories. Most gender systems are sex-based, with masculine, feminine, and sometimes neuter nouns. However, in some languages "gender" is based on other categories such as animate versus inanimate, human versus non-human, or even "vegetable" (Corbett 2013b). Another difference is that in some languages, gender agreement applies to verbs as well as adjectives and the like. Hebrew is one example of such a language.

*Teacher talk*

"Casi la mitad de los idiomas, igual al español, divide sus sustantivos ('nouns') en categorías como masculina y femenina. Unos tienen más de dos géneros, por ejemplo masculino, femenino y neutro."

*In-class activities*

- **Demonstrate the ubiquity of gender.** This exercise underscores the high proportion of words in Spanish text that are gendered. Each student needs a physical page of Spanish text, such as a printed newspaper article or a photocopied book page; this can either be the same or unique for each student. The task is to underline or highlight every gendered noun and every article, adjective, or pronoun that agrees with it, using contrasting colors for masculine and feminine. The colors used are up to the teacher and/or students, though pink and blue would be traditional. The proportion of underlined or highlighted words will be impressive. If desired, this proportion can then be quantified by counting the numbers of masculine and feminine words, compared to the total number of words, in the text(s).

  This activity can inspire some high-level thinking about gender. Should *el* before feminine nouns, as in *el agua*, be considered (and colored) masculine or feminine? Should invariant words, such as *-ista* nouns, *gran*, and possessive adjectives like *mi*, be considered neuter, or should they be interpreted in a gendered fashion according to context? For example, *mi* could be colored as feminine before *casa* but as masculine before *amigo* – or it could be passed over. The teacher can decide beforehand how students should handle these cases, or the class can discuss exactly what it means for a word to be masculine or feminine.

- **Use gender-distinguished word pairs.** Grammatical gender allows a single Spanish word form to have two meanings, depending on whether it is treated as masculine or feminine word (e.g. *el/la papa*). This activity calls students' attention to such word pairs, eight of which are listed in Slides 2.33 and 2.34 (the latter with meaning clues). Students write a sentence for each word pair, such as *El papa cultivaba papas*, and the class votes on the most original sentence for each word pair.

- **Explore the role of gender in fruit and tree names.** For a small subset of Spanish objects, gender is systematic rather than random. As shown in Slide 2.35, most feminine fruit names that end in -*a* correspond to tree names that end in -*o*. The vitality of this pattern shows in its application not only to Latinate words like *manzana*, but also to the borrowed words *banana* (West Africa), *frambuesa* (French), *lúcuma* (Quechua), and *naranja* and *aceituna* (Arabic). For a simple activity, the teacher can display the slide and ask students to volunteer the missing words.

  Slide 2.36 shows that tree names for masculine fruits are much more variable. Teachers might wish to point out that fruit and tree names can vary according to dialect; for example, *durazno* and *duraznero* are primarily used in Latin America, but *melocotón* and *melocotonero* are standard in Spain. (See "Vocabulary" in Chapter 4.)

- **Discuss or debate gender-neutral language.** Many people today, especially younger people, are concerned with perceived sexism in language. In English, such speakers object to the normative use of the masculine gender in sentences such as *A good student does <u>his</u> homework every night*. In Spanish, this issue arises most often with regard to plural forms that end in -*os*, as in the sentence *Ell<u>os</u> son l<u>os</u> cirujan<u>os</u> más talentos<u>os</u>*. From a grammatical perspective these forms are simply the normal way to refer to combined groups of men and women (or girls and boys). To the modern ear (and eye), they can seem biased toward the male sex – in this case, apparently excluding female surgeons.

  Many Spanish speakers today use alternative phrasings and spellings to avoid this perceived bias. They may expand a masculine plural like *ellos* into a conjoined phrase like *ellos y ellas*. This solution is most common in spoken Spanish, as conjoined phrases are bulky when written. As a second strategy they may replace the *o* in -*os* with the @ sign (*arroba*) or *x*, as in *ell@s* or *cirujanxs*. Such substitutions are also seen in the singular, as in the use of *latinx* (pronounced "latinex") for *latino* in the United States. Finally, speakers may avoid the plural entirely, for example replacing *los andaluces* with *el pueblo andaluz* or *todos los miembros* with *cada miembro* (examples from Tribunal de Cuentas 2020).

  Spanish language authorities, including the Real Academia Española, have continued to stand by the traditional forms, and actively oppose the use of conjoined phrases or spelling changes (@s or *xs*).

  Gender-neutral Spanish can be an engaging subject for a classroom discussion or debate because students are already familiar with this issue in English. Students can discuss or debate whether the traditional forms are in fact biased, and also consider the relative merits of the alternatives listed above. Teachers can catalyze the activity by sharing examples of -@s and -*xs* used in place of -*os* in public spaces, as in

Slide 2.37, and/or a short text about this topic, such as one of those listed in Slide 2.38. As a follow-up, students may write an essay summarizing their opinion on the question of gender-neutral Spanish, and/or do the take-home activity "Researching gender-neutral Spanish."

*Take-home projects*

- **Compare noun genders in Spanish and another language.** In this activity students compare the genders of a set of Spanish nouns, such as clothing terms or body parts, to the genders of the equivalent nouns in another language. They record their findings in a table, as shown in Slide 2.39. All students can look up the same words in the same language, or different students can work with different words and/or languages.

   This activity encourages students to step back from Spanish and think about gender more broadly. It primarily highlights the random nature of grammatical gender: few nouns are semantically masculine or feminine, so that the gender of a Spanish noun is not likely to carry over to another language. It also reminds students that other languages besides Spanish have grammatical gender. Finally, depending on the choice of the other language, it can show students that not all gender systems are based on a binary distinction between masculine and feminine nouns.

   Students can certainly compare Spanish with another Romance language. However, to reduce the number of cognates that have the same gender, such as Spanish *la boca* and French *la bouche*, teachers can steer students instead toward languages that belong to a different language family, such as German, Dutch, Polish, or Czech. Adding further interest, German, Polish, and Czech have three genders (masculine, feminine, and neuter), while Dutch has merged masculine and feminine into a single "common" gender in contrast to neuter. Hebrew, Arabic, Greek, or Russian would also be an excellent choice if a student happens to be familiar with one of these languages.

   Students should use a bilingual dictionary, either printed or online (such as wordreference.com), to look up the words and their genders. For the languages mentioned above, students will need to know that masculine, feminine and neuter nouns are labeled *m, f,* and *n* in German, *m, ż,* and *n* in Polish, and *m, ž,* and *s* in Czech; "common" and neuter Dutch nouns are indicated with *de* and *het*.
- **Research gender-neutral Spanish.** This activity extends, or could replace, the in-class activity "Discussing or debating gender-neutral language." Each student (or pair of students) reads a text about on non-sexist usage, such as those in Slide 2.38, summarizes its main argument and subarguments (perhaps using a graphical organizer), and shares this summary with the class. Students may enjoy finding their own texts on the

Internet; in this case, some useful search strings will be *arroba género, español no sexista,* and *español neutro en cuanto al género.*

For a deeper dive into the topic, students can read and summarize a manual of non-sexist language practices such as Tribunal de Cuentas (2020), UPM (2020), or Quilis Merín, Albelda Marco, and Cuenca (2012). The first of these is governmental and the latter two are academic. An appropriate summary might include examples of the recommended practices along with the student's reactions to each of them. Are the practices feasible? Will they result in stilted or otherwise poor writing? Depending on the length of the manual, students might share this task; in that case they should meet to review and evaluate the practices together.

### The personal a

#### Just the facts

The personal *a* is yet another feature of Spanish that is lacking in English yet has parallels in many other languages. It is what linguists call a "differential object marker": a word (or affix) that accompanies direct objects that have the characteristics of a typical subject, such as being human and specific (Slide 2.40). According to Bossong (1991), over three hundred languages employ a differential object marker; Slide 2.41 shows some examples.

For an English-speaking student already put off by the alien nature of the personal *a,* a second pedagogical challenge is that it often appears unnecessary: in simple sentences like *Visito a mi amiga* it could be eliminated without any loss of meaning. For this reason it is helpful to point out to students other sentence types in which the personal *a* plays a vital role in distinguishing subject and object. Essentially, these are sentences that go against standard subject-verb-object word order, either for stylistic reasons or to form a question (Slides 2.42 and 2.43).

#### Teacher talk

"Cientos de idiomas usan una palabra como la *a* personal para identificar objetos gramaticales que no son típicos porque tienen las características de sujetos – por ejemplo, porque son personas específicas. En español la *a* personal nos ayuda a distinguir entre sujetos y objetos en ciertas frases, y por eso la usamos siempre."

#### Take-home projects

- **Push the boundaries of the personal *a*.** In this activity students create and illustrate improbable sentences with objects that require the personal *a,* such as *El libro comió al niño* and *La manzana buscó a Elena.* Students can either illustrate their sentences themselves or find (or construct) the illustrations online. One way to organize this project is for students to add their illustrated sentences to an online album that other students then view and comment on. Students might score each sentence for *originalidad* and *ilustración*.

- **Write a quiz using *¿Quién(es)?* and *¿A quién(es)?*** This activity reinforces the importance of the personal *a* in questions that have a human subject and a human object. Each student (or pair of students) writes a quiz in which each question begins with *¿Quién(es)?* or *¿A quién(es)?* The quiz can either be personal (e.g. *¿A quién admiras más?*) or historical (e.g. *¿Quién asesinó al emperor Maximiliano?*). Either quiz type should contain roughly an equal number of *Quién(es)* and *A quién(es)* questions; historical quizzes should be multiple-choice. Slides 2.44 and 2.45 list suggested verbs for the two themes.

  When assessing the quizzes teachers should be particularly alert for uses of *A quién(es)* that are indirect rather than personal, for example *¿A quiénes les das un regalo de cumpleaños?* Once students correct their quizzes based on teacher feedback, they can exchange quizzes in class and answer the questions.

The following references are cited in this chapter's text and/or its accompanying PowerPoint presentation.

## References

Bossong, G. 1991. Differential object marking in Romance and beyond. In *New analyses in Romance linguistics*, eds. D. Kibbee and D. Wanner, 143–70. Amsterdam: John Benjamins.

Corbett, G. G. 2013a. Number of genders. In Dryer and Haspelmath 2013, ch. 30.

———. 2013b. Systems of gender assignment. In Dryer and Haspelmath 2013, ch. 32.

Dahl, O., and V. Velupillai. 2013. Perfective/imperfective aspect. In Dryer and Haspelmath 2013, ch. 65.

Davies, M. 2006. *A frequency dictionary of Spanish*. Routledge Frequency Dictionaries. London: Routledge.

Davies, M., and D. Gardner. 2010. *A frequency dictionary of contemporary American English*. Routledge Frequency Dictionaries. London: Routledge.

de Swart, P. 2006. Case markedness. In *Case, valency and transitivity*, eds. L. Kulikov, A. Malchukov, and P. de Swart, 249–68. Philadelphia, PA: John Benjamins.

de Swart, P., and H. de Hoop. 2007. Semantic aspects of differential object marking. In *Proceedings of Sinn und Bedeutung 11*, ed. E. Puig-Waldmüller, 598–611. Barcelona: Universitat Pompeu Fabra.

Dryer, M. S., and M. Haspelmath, eds. 2013. The world atlas of language structures online. Leipzig: Max Planck Institute for Evolutionary Anthropology. http://wals.info.

Gurlekian, J. A., N. Elisei, and M. Eleta. 2004. Caracterización articulatoria de los sonidos vocálicos del español de Buenos Aires mediante técnicas de resonancia magnética. *Revista Fonoaudiológica* (ASALFA: Asociación Argentina de Logopedia, Foniatría y Audiología): 50(2): 7–14.

Helmbrecht, J. 2013. Politeness distinctions in pronouns. In Dryer and Haspelmath 2013, ch. 45.

Ingram, D. 1978. Typology and universals of personal pronouns. In *Universals of Human Language*, ed. J. H. Greenberg, Vol. 3, 213–48. Stanford, CA: Stanford University Press.

Juegosdepalabras. 2020. Palabras panvocálicas o pentavocálicas ordenadas por orden alfabético. *Juegos de palabras.* https://www.juegosdepalabras.com/vocales/panvocalicas-2.html.

Maddieson, I. 2009. *Patterns of sounds*. Cambridge: Cambridge University Press.

———. 2013. Syllable structure. In Dryer and Haspelmath 2013, ch. 12.

Quilis Merín, M., M. Albelda Marco, and M. J. Cuenca. 2012. *Guía del uso para un lenguaje igualitario (castellano)*. Valencia: Univ. de València. https://www.uv.es/igualtat/GUIA/GUIA_CAS.pdf.

Rusch, D., M. Domínguez, and L. Caycedo Garner. 2007. *Imágenes: An introduction to Spanish language and cultures, Teacher's edition*. Boston, MA: Houghton Mifflin.

Schwartz, J-L., L-J. Boë, N. Vallée, and C. Abry. 1997. Major trends in vowel system inventories. *Journal of Phonetics* 25: 233–53.

Stassen, L. 2013. Nominal and locational predication. In Dryer and Haspelmath 2013, ch. 119.

Tomasena, M. 2020. Cómo decidir si escribir de tú o de usted en la web de tu negocio. *Maïder Tomasena: Done el copywriting genera resultados.* https://www.maidertomasena.com/como-decidir-si-escribir-de-tu-o-de-usted-en-la-web-de-tu-negocio/.

Tribunal de Cuentas. 2020. *Sugerencias para uso no sexista del lenguaje administrativo del tribunal de cuentas.* https://www.tcu.es/tribunal-de-cuentas/export/sites/default/.content/pdf/Sugerencias-para-uso-no-sexista-del-lenguaje-administrativo-del-TCu.pdf.

UPM. 2020. *Manual de lenguaje no sexista en la Universiad Politécnica de Madrid.* http://www.upm.es/sfs/Rectorado/Gerencia/Igualdad/Lenguaje/MANUAL_DE_LENGUAJE_NO_SEXISTA_EN_LA_UPM.pdf.

# Chapter 3

# What are the roots of Spanish?

Students benefit in two ways when they learn about the roots of Spanish. First, language history is interesting in and of itself. The "external history" of Spanish – the chain of world events that shaped its growth – is a dramatic tale of conquests, reconquests, and mass migrations, each of which left its imprint on the modern language. It also establishes the privileged status of Spanish as a member of the world's largest language family (Indo-European) and as part of the legacy of the Roman Empire. The "internal history" of Spanish – the changes in pronunciation, vocabulary, and grammar that the language underwent as it evolved – is of intellectual interest as well. A good example is the topic of semantic change. It is fascinating to learn that, for example, *infante* once referred to all children, not just royals, and that *casa* has been upgraded from a 'hut' to a 'house.'

At the same time, the roots of Spanish can often shine light on confusing aspects of modern-day Spanish. For example, the irregular form *conozco* simply reflects the verb's original Latin infinitive, *cognoscere*. The extreme irregularity of *ir* and *ser* arose, in large part, because each of these verbs combines three distinct roots. As a non-verb example, *para* began as *por* plus *a*, an origin that explains the directional aspect of many uses of *para*.

This chapter begins with a bird's-eye view of the external history of Spanish, then moves step by step through this narrative, from the Indo-European conquest of Italy to modern times. The second part of the chapter focuses on the internal history of Spanish, covering the evolution of Spanish sounds, words, and grammar.

The in-class activities in this chapter fall into two general categories. Some have students tap into and build on their **existing knowledge**. For example, in one activity students guesstimate the boundaries of the Roman Empire on a map and compare these with the actual boundaries. Other activities encourage students to work with **language data** hands-on: for example, classifying Spanish words of Arabic origin by their semantic category (architecture, agriculture, and so on), or analyzing the complex irregularities of *ir* and *ser* to discover their three roots. Most of the chapter's take-home projects are **structured research tasks**, such as looking up the pre-Roman origins of Spanish place names or categorizing a list of words ending in *-ma* according to their origin (Greek or not) and gender. For a full list of the chapter's activities and projects, and their suitability for different levels of instruction, see Appendices A and B.

For additional historical perspectives, see the sections on the inverted *¡* and *¿* marks, the *eñe*, and the two forms of the imperfect subjunctive in Chapter 1, and the sections on the multiple 'you' pronouns and the verb *estar* in Chapter 2.

## External history

### A bird's-eye view of the history of Spanish

*Just the facts*

The modern Spanish language is the product of a dramatic series of conquests (Slide 3.1). The first of these was the Indo-European conquest of Italy around 1000 BCE, where the Roman version of proto-Indo-European eventually evolved into Latin. The second was the Roman conquest of the Iberian Peninsula, beginning in 206 BCE. With the fall of the Roman Empire, the Visigoths, a Germanic tribe, took control of the Peninsula by 475 CE, only to be themselves vanquished in 711 by the Moors (Arab-led Berbers from North Africa). From then until 1492 the Christians slowly recaptured the Peninsula, proceeding from north to south, and beginning in that year Spain itself conquered large parts of the Americas.

From a linguistic perspective, the most important of these conquests by far was the first, because Spanish remains fundamentally an Indo-European language. It is true that Spanish absorbed much vocabulary as a result of the subsequent conquests, especially Arabic words. However, as far as linguists have been able to determine, neither Arabic, nor any of the other languages with which Spanish interacted during its formative centuries, significantly affected Spanish pronunciation or grammar.

*Teacher talk*

"El español es el fruto de una larga serie de conquistas. Para empezar, los ancianos indo-europeos conquistaron Italia, y luego los romanos conquistaron la península ibérica, trayendo consigo el latín. Cuando cayó el Imperio Romano, primero los visigodos y luego los moros conquistaron la península. Hasta 1492 los cristianos iban reconquistándola, uniendo el país, y entonces España empezó a conquistar Latinoamérica."

*In-class activity*

* **Trace the chronology of Spanish.** Slide 3.2 lists the main historical events (*conquistas*) described above, but out of order. Using common sense and/or resources available in the classroom, students attempt to put these events in

the correct order and assign each a date or date range. The teacher can then show the actual chronology (Slide 3.3 or again Slide 3.1).

*Take-home project*

- **Create a class timeline of the history of Spanish.** Students (or pairs of students) are each assigned one of the historical events listed in Slide 3.3. They each create a poster, or a presentation slide, about "their" phase of Spanish history. The poster or slide should identify the event and when it happened, and include an image that sums it up, a slogan or question that encapsulates it, and a color or colors that represent(s) it. Slide 3.4 is an example slide from American history; a click identifies the five required elements. Students then present their poster or slide to the class and explain their choices.

## Spanish as an Indo-European language

*Just the facts*

Spanish, along with the other Romance languages, is part of the Indo-European family of languages (Slide 3.5). This is the most important language family in the world, consisting of almost 450 languages spoken by more than three billion people living in over sixty countries (Eberhard, Simons, and Fennig 2020). As shown with a red X on the map, the Indo-European family originated in the Pontiac-Caspian steppes north of the Black and Caspian Seas, an area that spans Ukraine, southern Russia, and Kazakhstan (Fortson 2010, 46). In prehistoric times it spread throughout Europe and into the Near East and South Asia, and in the modern era has continued to advance into the Americas, Australia, and Africa. Besides the Romance languages, widely spoken Indo-European languages include Germanic languages such as English, Slavic languages such as Russian, North Indian languages such as Hindi, and Near Eastern languages such as Persian.

Many linguistic features of Spanish are typically Indo-European. These include basic features of the language such as noun gender, the language's large inventory of consonants, and its rich system of verb tenses and moods. A subtler feature is that word endings simultaneously express multiple facets of meaning. For example, *-iste* expresses second person, singular number, completive past tense, and indicative mood. In some non-Indo-European languages such as Hungarian, each bit of meaning is instead encoded in a separate word ending or other unit of speech.

*Teacher talk*

"El español pertenece a la familia de lenguajes más importante del mundo, los idiomas indo-europeos. Esta familia está compuesta de casi 450 idiomas hablados por más de tres mil millones (3.000.000.000) de personas. Además de los lenguajes romances, la familia indo-europea incluye lenguajes importantes como el inglés, el ruso, el hindi y la persa. Muchos aspectos fundamentales del español, como el género (nombres masculinos y femeninos), son típicos de los idiomas indo-europeos."

*In-class activities*

- **Identify Indo-European languages**. Students work through a list of the twenty-five most spoken languages of the world (Slide 3.6) and provisionally identify each as Romance, other Indo-European, or non-Indo-European. Afterward, they compare their work first with another student, and then with the correct identifications in Slide 3.7, or as grouped in Slide 3.8.
- **Group languages based on the numbers 1–10**. This activity gives students the opportunity to "play historical linguist" by hypothesizing historical language groups on the basis of modern language data. In preparation for this activity the teacher should print the table embedded in Slide 3.9, which lists the numbers 1–10 in twenty-four languages. Each student (or pair of students) will need a copy of this document, which the teacher or students should cut into twenty-four pieces. Students then group these into Romance languages, other Indo-European languages, and non-Indo-European languages, based on the numbers' similarity to Spanish, English, and any other languages they are familiar with. Afterward, the teacher can present the correct answers in Slide 3.10. This slide is animated so that the teacher can reveal the groupings, as well as the identities of the languages, click by click as students share their own answers.
- **Infer Indo-European culture.** The Indo-European people brought their culture with them along with their language as they spread through Europe and beyond. This activity challenges students to think about what we can infer about this culture based on linguistic evidence. It can begin with a general discussion: what do languages, and especially vocabulary, tell us about culture? What categories of words might we examine in order to learn about a culture? How can we reasonably determine which words were part of the original Indo-European language (Proto-Indo-European), not developed later or borrowed from other language families? These questions are expressed in Spanish in Slide 3.11. Teachers should guide the class to the conclusion that words that are shared by many modern Indo-European languages, in form and in meaning, are likely to have been present in Proto-Indo-European as well.

  Slide 3.12 then illustrates several such words that touch on Indo-European agriculture, social structure, technology, and religion, restricting the comparison to Spanish and English. The class should discuss these example words and what they imply about Indo-European culture. For example, the invention of the chariot helped the Indo-Europeans to spread out from their original homeland. Slide 3.13 contains a longer list of such words, not organized thematically, that students can analyze on their own, then use as the basis for a paragraph on "Qué sabemos de la cultura indo-europea por sus palabras."

### Take-home project

• **Color-code a map of the Indo-European region.** The goal of this activity is to impress students with the enormity and variety of the Indo-European language family, while demonstrating the size and location of Spanish and the other Romance languages relative to this family as a whole. Students color-code an online or printed map of Europe, the Near East, and South Asia to show whether each country's primary language is Romance, otherwise Indo-European, or non-Indo-European. Students should work from the list of languages and countries in Slide 3.14, checking off each country as they color-code it on the map, using the colors on the slide or choosing others.

  Students can do this task either online, using a website such as map-chart.net, or on paper, using a printed outline map such as the one in Slide 3.15. (Some map options may lack Monaco, Andorra, and Luxembourg, the smaller countries included in Slide 3.14.) If students work online, they should submit a screen shot of their finished map for assessment. Slide 3.16 shows an example.

  In a follow-up discussion, the teacher should remind students that the countries on the map are merely the home base of the Indo-European language family, which has also taken over Australia, the Americas, and parts of Africa. The teacher should also point out that besides the three non-Indo-European languages of Western Europe (Finnish, Hungarian, and Estonian), Basque is spoken in northern Spain and southern France (see Chapter 4).

### Spain before Latin

#### Just the facts

When the Romans arrived in the Iberian Peninsula in the third century BCE, they found a variety of peoples already living there, speaking a variety of languages (Slide 3.17). We know about these languages from Roman records and other contemporary accounts, from written inscriptions, and from the vocabulary and place names the pre-Roman peoples left behind. Of course, other languages may have been spoken in the Peninsula without leaving a trace.

Of the six languages (or language groups) shown in Slide 3.17, three had been present in the Peninsula since prehistoric times:

- Aquitanian, the forerunner to today's Basque, was spoken in the north. For simplicity's sake, it is labeled as *vasco* in this section's slides.
- Iberian was spoken primarily in the east. Historians know about this language only from mentions in contemporary accounts and several undecipherable inscriptions.
- Tartessian, known only from contemporary mentions, was spoken mostly in today's Portugal but also in neighboring parts of today's Spain.

Three other languages (or language groups) were more recent arrivals, the first by land and the others by sea:

- Celtic languages, sometimes called "Celtiberian," were Indo-European languages related to today's Breton, Welsh, Irish, and Scottish Gaelic. They were spoken in the peninsula's interior, especially the north.
- Greek was found in trading settlements on the Eastern coast.
- Phoenician, the Semitic language of Carthage in northern Africa, was widely spoken on the Mediterranean coast and islands.

*Teacher talk*

"Cuando llegaron los romanos a la península ibérica en el tercer siglo antes de la era común, encontraron a varias gentes que ya vivían allí y hablaban varios idiomas de diferentes familias lingüísticas. Sabemos de estos idiomas por descripciones romanas, por inscripciones antiguas, y por el vocabulario que contribuyeron al español."

*In-class activities*

- **Surprise students with pre-Roman vocabulary.** This activity is a way to introduce the topic of pre-Roman languages "from scratch." Slide 3.18 shows several common Spanish words borrowed from pre-Roman languages other than Greek and Phoenician. The instructor should ask students to work with a partner to guess which languages these words were borrowed from based on their sound and meaning, perhaps noting their predictions on a copy of the slide. They may guess languages like French, Italian, and Arabic. The instructor (or a student) can then compile students' guesses so that the class can compare them to the words' actual origins, which are color-coded on the next slide (Slide 3.19). This revelation would segue naturally into a presentation of Slide 3.17, and a discussion of why Latin borrowed these particular words: what do they say about the relationship between the natives of Iberian Peninsula and their Roman conquerors?

A class discussion can also touch on certain words in this activity that are of particular interest. *Izquierda* is the most notable from a linguistic perspective. For one thing, it is the one Spanish word that all experts agree is Basque in origin, leaving aside modern borrowings like *boina* (Trask 1997, 415–21). Additionally, this borrowing displaced *sinister*, the original Latin word for 'left.' Scholars believe that *sinister* was ripe for replacement because it had developed a negative connotation, just like French *gauche* (Penny 2002, 256). Finally, some of the Celtic words (*camino, camisa, carpintero,* and *carro*) are not native to the Iberian Peninsula: Romans borrowed them from Celtic speakers in Gaul (today's France), then imported them into Spain.

- **Categorize pre-Roman vocabulary.** This activity is an alternative to the previous one ("Surprising students with pre-Roman vocabulary"). The Romans borrowed native words for local plants (e.g. *álamo*), animals (e.g. *sapo*), and everyday objects (e.g. *carro*), as well as other useful words. In this activity students explore this phase of the language's history by dividing a group of words of pre-Roman origin into the semantic categories shown in Slide 3.20. This can be either the thirty-six words in Slides 3.21 or 3.22 (with and without translations) or the subset of twenty-six words in Slide 3.23, which are either basic (e.g. *camino*) or illustrated. Afterward, the class can discuss which semantic categories are largest and why.

    See the notes above on *izquierda* and on Celtic words of Gaulish origin, to which this activity adds *legua* (Slides 3.21 and 3.22 only) and *cabaña*. An additional word of cultural interest is *madroño* 'strawberry tree,' which appears with a bear on Madrid's coat of arms and in other symbols of the city (see illustration in Slide 3.23).

## Take-home project

- **Research pre-Roman place names.** The goal of this project is to acquaint students with the variety and location of pre-Roman languages and cultures. Working from and annotating the map in Slide 3.24, students look up the pre-Roman origins of the names of more than a dozen selected locations in Spain, including *España* itself. As indicated on that slide, these toponyms (place names) all come from Basque, Iberian, Greek, Celtic (sometimes called "Celtiberian"), or Phoenician (also called "Carthaginian"). Slide 3.25 shows the actual origins.

    Wikipedia is an adequate resource for this project; students should look for name origins under "etymology," "name(s)," or "history." Ulaca is found only on Spanish Wikipedia. To add more cultural interest, students can find and share illustrations of these locations.

### The Roman conquest

*Just the facts*

Rome conquered the Iberian Peninsula gradually. The conquest started with Rome's victory over Carthage in southern Spain in 206 BCE as part of the second Punic War, and ended under Emperor Augustus in 19 BCE. The Empire would continue to advance further into Europe as well as the Near East and Northern Africa (Slide 3.26), giving rise to the Romance language family in much of this territory.

The Roman soldiers and colonists who settled in the Peninsula did not speak Classical Latin, but rather Vulgar Latin, the Latin of the common people. For the most part, linguists have inferred the characteristics of this language from commonalities among the Romance languages. For example, every Romance language has a past tense based on the verb 'to have,' such as the Spanish present perfect (e.g. *he hablado*), so Vulgar Latin probably did as well. However, there is some direct written evidence in the form of graffiti, informal letters, the speech of rustic characters in Latin plays, and pedagogical corrections (Slide 3.28).

*Teacher talk*

"La conquista del territorio que hoy es España empezó en el año 206 a.C, y duró hasta el año 19 a.C. Los romanos que se instalaron en este territorio no hablaban el latín clásico, sino el latín vulgar. Esta no fue una lengua escrita, por lo cual la conocemos mayormente por las características de los idiomas romances que vinieron de ella."

*In-class activities*

*   **Guesstimate the boundaries of the Roman Empire.** This activity gives students the chance to find out for themselves the size of the Roman Empire. The teacher should first project the unmarked map of Europe in Slide 3.27 onto a whiteboard or other writeable surface. Then different students volunteer (or are volunteered) to come to the board and draw what they believe to be the Empire's borders, ideally each with a different-colored marker. The teacher should then display Slide 3.26 so students can compare their boundaries with the actual ones.
*   **Who can name the most Romance languages?** In this simple activity, students or pairs of students write down the Romance languages they know of. The student (pair) with the most languages shares their list. Other students/pairs can add additional languages to help the class arrive at a definitive list. At this point the teacher can display Slide 3.29, which maps the principal Romance languages (it omits others such

as Provençal and Sardinian). Since this map includes Galician and Catalan, it can lead to a discussion of what distinguishes a language from a dialect; the teacher may want to share Max Weinreich's (1945) dictum that "a language is a dialect with an army and a navy."

- **Identify Romance languages.** This activity gives students an impression of the range of linguistic variation within the Romance family. Slide 3.30 contains written translations of the beginning of the Universal Declaration of Human Rights; for spoken examples, Slide 3.31 contains links to a variety of YouTube clips. In both cases, teachers should give students the chance to read (or listen to) the materials and guess the languages before identifying them.
- **Brainstorm sources of evidence for Vulgar Latin.** The Romans left an extensive body of literature in Classical Latin, from plays and poetry to essays and letters, and even study materials for Greeks who wanted to learn Latin. In contrast, Vulgar Latin (the immediate source of the Spanish language) was primarily a spoken language. How, then, can we know what it was like?

  In this activity, groups of students brainstorm about the types of evidence that might exist to help us learn about Vulgar Latin, then share their ideas with the rest of the class. The teacher can show Slide 3.28 as a wrap-up.

### Take-home projects

- **Research Romance demographics.** In this WebQuest, students go online to find basic information about the principal Romance languages, such as the number and location of their speakers, and record their answers in a table like the one embedded in Slide 3.32. Wikipedia is an acceptable resource for this activity. As part of this activity or as a follow-up, each student could write down and share three new facts of general interest they learned when doing the activity.
- **Profile a Romance language.** Students, or pairs of students, each profile a Romance language other than Spanish. These can be limited to the seven shown in Slide 3.29 or extended to smaller Romance languages such as Provençal, Sardinian, Gascon, Asturian, and Ladino. The profile should contain the elements listed in Slide 3.33, and can be in the form of a poster, slide presentation, or oral report that can be shared with the class.

## After Rome

### Just the facts

As Rome fell, the Visigoths and other Germanic tribes moved south into former Roman territory. The Visigoths conquered Spain by the year 475 and established Toledo as their capital. Some Visigothic words entered Spanish as a result of this invasion; others had already been absorbed into Vulgar Latin, and so can be found in other Romance languages as well as Spanish. Besides Visigothic, other Germanic languages such as Frankish (the language that gave its name to France) contributed vocabulary to Spanish. Germanic words in Spanish generally pertain to war (e.g. *guerra*), horsemanship (e.g. *látigo*), or everyday life (e.g. *rico*). Slide 3.34 presents several words of Visigothic and other Germanic origin.

The Visigothic period in Spain ended in 711 when the Moors – Arab-led Berbers from North Africa – crossed the Straits of Gilbraltar to conquer most of the Iberian Peninsula. Just as the Visigothic conquest was part of the fall of Rome, so too the Moorish conquest was part of a larger historical movement: the territorial expansion of Islam. The original conquerors were followed by additional Arab settlers, making Arabic a predominant language of the Peninsula. Christians living in Arab-held territory continued to speak the local form of early Romance, somewhat confusingly called Mozarabic. Some churches in Spain continue to offer Mass in this language.

During this period Spanish absorbed a great deal of Arabic vocabulary (Slide 3.35). These words mostly pertain to specific semantic domains such as government (e.g. *alcalde*) and agriculture (e.g. *zanahoria*). Many words of Arabic origin, such as *alcalde*, begin with *al-*, the Arabic word for 'the.' The article was borrowed along with the words themselves, just as English would later borrow *el lagarto* from Spanish as *alligator*. Another common feature in Arabic borrowings is an *h* between two vowels (as in *zahahoria*), which sometimes replaced a hard-to-pronounce Arabic consonant. Some words, such as *alcohol* and *almohada*, have both of these features.

### Teacher talk

"Dos grupos conquistaron España al fin del Empirio Romano: primero los visigodos, una tribu germánica, en 475, y luego los moros, quienes hablaban árabe, en 711. El español adquirió muchas palabras de estos dos grupos, sobre todo de los moros. El vocabulario de origen visigodo por lo general tiene que ver con la guerra y con la equitación. El vocabulario árabe forma una parte importante del español y tiene que ver con muchos temas, incluso el gobierno y la agricultura. Muchas palabras árabes, como *alcalde* y *alfombra*, empiezan con *al*, la palabra árabe que quiere decir *el* o *la*."

### In-class activities

- **Categorize Germanic vocabulary.** This activity introduces students to a core set of Spanish words of Germanic origin and the semantic classes they belong to. Students simply divide the words listed in Slide 3.34, which includes illustrations of some less-familiar words, into the categories shown in Slide 3.36.

*   **Categorize Arabic vocabulary.** This is the same as the activity above, but involves words of Arabic rather than Germanic origin and a different set of semantic categories (Slides 3.35 and 3.37).
*   **Arabic or not?** Many – but not all – Spanish words that begin with *al-*, or have an *h* between two vowels, are of Arabic origin. This activity asks students to predict which of a set of words with one or both of these characteristics come from Arabic, and which do not. The words and answers are in Slides 3.38 and 3.39.

This is not a guessing activity; students should make use of what they have learned about the semantics of typical Arabic loanwords (Slide 3.37), and also common sense. For example, *alma* and *buho* do not fit into any of the typical Arabic categories such as agriculture and commerce. *Alcanzar* and *prohibir* are verbs whereas most Arabic borrowings (like borrowings in general) are nouns. *Alpaca* and *chihuahua* are creatures of the New World, not northern Africa. The real surprise on this list is *almendra*. It appears to be an Arabic loanword because it begins with *al-* and describes a food cultivated in the Middle East, but it is in fact of Greek origin (via Latin).

## The Reconquista

### Just the facts

The Reconquista was the centuries-long war in which the Christian forces of northern Spain took back the rest of the peninsula from its Arabic-speaking conquerors. It established Castilian Spanish, the primary language of those forces (including El Cid), as the standard form of Spanish. As *castellano* swept south, it continued to absorb Arabic words from speakers of Arabic and Mozarabic, which had incorporated much Arabic vocabulary. The Reconquista culminated in 1492 with the taking of Granada, the expulsion of the Jews, and Columbus's sailing to America.

One consequence of the Reconquista is that Spain differs from other European countries in the source of its standard language. English, France, and Russian are based on the speech of their corresponding capital cities (London, Paris, and Moscow); Italian and German are based on the writings of Dante and Martin Luther. Only standard Spanish originated in a peripheral population center and spread via military conquest.

### Teacher talk

"Desde 711, cuando los moros conquistaron la península ibérica, los cristianos del norte de España lucharon para reconquistar este territorio. Esta lucha continuó hasta 1492, cuando el ejército del rey Ferdinand y la reina Isabela conquistó Granada, la última ciudad española baja el control árabe. Los cristianos trajeron con ellos el castellano: la variedad del español hablada en la región de Castilla, en el norte de España. Así el castellano llegó a ser la forma estándar del español."

*In-class activity*

- **Observe the spread of *castellano* via animation.** The GIF in Slide 3.40 (Vigo 2009) recapitulates the spread of Castilian Spanish between the years 1000 and 2000, with the greatest detail in the Reconquista years. The teacher can show the GIF several times so that students can take notes on several aspects: the spread of *castellano*, the shrinking territory of Arabic and Mozarabic, and then the continued expansion of *castellano* at the expense of other varieties of Hispanic Romance. Students can also observe Galician spreading south to give rise to Portuguese.

  As a caveat, this GIF contains some glaring inaccuracies, such as an enormous footprint for Occitan in modern-day Southern France. Nevertheless it is a useful way to capture the downward sweep of Castilian at the expense of competing forms of Spanish Romance.

*Take-home project*

- **Compare *castellano* to other European language standards.** In this WebQuest (Slide 3.41), students research the source of the standard forms of different European languages. As noted above, they should find that with the exception of Spanish, these standards came from either capital cities or landmark authors. Besides the languages mentioned above, the WebQuest includes Danish, Swedish, Portuguese, and Catalan, all of whose standards come from capital cities, Dutch, whose standard comes from Antwerp (a major city though not a capital), and Finnish, whose standard is based on the author Elias Lönnrot. The slide supplies answers for German and English as models.

## Spanish comes to the Americas

*Just the facts*

Spain began its conquest of the Americas in 1492, seeking a sea route to Asia and any treasure Columbus could find along the way. The Spanish crown also saw this enterprise as a continuation of the Reconquista, an opportunity to win new souls to Catholicism. Columbus and his successors never found the sea route they were looking for, but they returned ample treasure to the Spanish coffers and converted a multitude of indigenous Americans.

Spain's first foothold in the Americas was the Caribbean islands, followed by colonial capitals in Mexico City and Lima. During the first centuries of Spanish dominion, the areas farthest from these capitals – specifically, the interior of Central America and the Atlantic coast of South America, including Buenos Aires (today a sophisticated, European-style city) – remained backwaters, reachable only by difficult land transportation through the jungle or across the Andes. This would have important dialectal consequences (see Chapter 4).

Whereas Basque was the only pre-Roman language of Spain to survive the advent of Latin, hundreds of indigenous languages of Latin America, from dozens of distinct language families, survived the coming of Spanish. This occurred because the newcomers were relatively few in number and were mostly men who intermarried with the native population. Nevertheless, more than half the original indigenous languages were lost as war, slavery, and disease devastated the indigenous population.

Spanish borrowed many words from the indigenous languages of Latin America, mostly to describe the local flora and fauna (e.g. *maíz* and *jaguar*). The colonists also adapted existing Spanish words to suit their new environment; for example, they extended *piña* to mean 'pineapple' as well as 'pine cone' and changed the meaning of *pavo* to 'turkey' from 'peacock' (now *pavo real*).

In Chapter 4, see the section "Spanish dialects" for the Andalusian origins of Latin American Spanish, and "Multilingualism in Latin America" for more about indigenous languages and their status today.

### Teacher talk

"La conquista de Latinoamérica empezó en 1492 con el primer viaje de Cristóbal Colón. Salió en búsqueda de una ruta marítima a Asia, de tesoro, y de almas a convertir al catolicismo. Colón llegó primero a lo que hoy es la República Dominicana. Luego vinieron otros conquistadores, y dentro de cuarenta años España había establecido capitales coloniales en la Ciudad de México y en Lima. Millones de indígenas murieron durante y después de la conquista, y también desaparecieron la mitad de los idiomas indígenas. Sin embargo sobrevivieron cientos de idiomas indígenas que todavía sirven hoy de primer idioma para millones de personas. Los idiomas indígenas también contribuyeron muchas palabras importantes al español, incluso palabras de comidas como el *chocolate* y de animales como el *jaguar*."

### In-class activity

- **Learn from a *conquista* quiz.** Working alone or in pairs or groups, and with or without access to Internet resources, students take the quiz embedded in Slide 3.42. (The quiz could also serve as a take-home

WebQuest.) The quiz uses color to indicate correct answers for reference purposes. Teachers should remove this coloring before distributing the quiz, and they may also choose to edit and/or reformat the quiz.

The individual questions in the quiz can be a springboard for class discussion. For example, why did the indigenous languages of the Caribbean die out while others survived? The names, places, and events in the quiz can also serve as topics for student research or presentations.

*Take-home project*

- **Research New World etymologies.** In this activity, students use the online dictionary of the Real Academia Española (rae.es) to learn about words that Spanish borrowed from indigenous languages of Latin America (Slide 3.43). Some of these words came from the Caribbean, some from Mexico, some from Peru and the Andes, and some from Paraguay. Slide 3.43 includes a list of the indigenous languages from each region that students will see on the rae.es website. The actual word origins are listed in Slide 3.44.

  The teacher may have each student (or group of students) look up the origins of the words in Slide 3.43 and write down each word in the correct region of the map in Slide 3.45. An alternative is to divide the four geographical areas (Caribbean, Mexico, Peru/Andes, and Paraguay) among different students (or groups). Each student (or group) first identifies the words from their assigned region, then creates a poster or presentation that illustrates the words.

  In any case, each regional cluster of words will serve as a capsule introduction to the flora, fauna, and (to some extent) human culture of that region. This could spark a class discussion or other follow-up activity.

## Modern times

*Just the facts*

While the dramatic series of conquests described above has come to an end, the evolution of Spanish has not. However, the pace of phonological and grammatical change has slowed down due to a combination of language standardization and mass communication. In fact, the main changes in phonology and grammar during this time period all happened early on, during the sixteenth and seventeenth centuries: the reduction of six Old Spanish sibilants to two (three in Castile), as described in the following section, and the creation of *usted* and *ustedes* ("Multiple *you* pronouns" in Chapter 2) and the -*ra* imperfect subjunctive ("The two imperfect subjunctives" in Chapter 1). Subsequent phonological and grammatical developments have mostly been smaller in scale and dialectal in scope. As discussed in Chapter 4, these include the continued weakening and loss of consonants at the end of syllables or between vowels, and variations in pronoun and verb tense usage. An important consequence of this evolutionary slowdown is that today, more than five hundred years after Spanish began its worldwide dispersion, most of its speakers can understand each other readily regardless of their origin.

In contrast to Spanish phonology and grammar, Spanish vocabulary has continued to evolve dynamically. Many new words, such as *parabrisas*, were created using the language itself as a resource. Others continued the medieval tradition of drawing on Latin, as discussed later in this chapter ("Sources of Spanish words"). An example is *progreso*, from Latin *progressus*, first attested in 1570 (Corominas 1973, 477). Finally, Spanish has continued to borrow from other languages. French was the main source of borrowings during most of the modern era, until English surpassed it in the twentieth century, reflecting the growing cultural, technological, and military prestige of the United States.

Modern times have also seen exciting changes in the status of the Spanish language. One is the growing importance, in both population and prestige, of Latin American Spanish. As with Portuguese, whose speech population is now dominated by Brazil, Spanish is now mostly spoken in the Americas. While peninsular Spanish retains to some extent its traditional prestige (see "Spanish dialects" in Chapter 4), the importance of Latin American Spanish and its speakers is reflected in Spanish literature, linguistics (from dictionaries to research papers), and language instruction, at least in the United States. These speakers have also pushed Spanish into its current position as the second most-spoken language in the world, as discussed in Chapter 1. Finally, Spanish has become by far the most popular language for second-language study in the United States. According to the Modern Language Association, Spanish enrollment in institutions of higher learning is greater than that of all other languages combined (Looney and Lusin 2019, 4).

## Teacher talk

"En los siglos más recientes el español ha continuado a crecer y cambiar. Por ejemplo, se perdieron unos sonidos, como la *z*, y se crearon otros: la *th* castellana y la *jota* pan-hispana. También se crearon los pronombres *usted* y *ustedes*. En cuanto a su vocabulario, el español continuó absorbiendo palabras de otros idiomas, sobre todo el francés y, empezando en el siglo veinte, el inglés. Finalmente, con el gran crecimiento de la población latinoamericana el español ha llegado a ser el segundo idioma más hablado del mundo, y el idioma extranjero más estudiado en los Estados Unidos."

*In-class activity*

Besides the activity below, see also "Find semantic patterns in borrowed words" in the section "Sources of Spanish words" later in this chapter.

- **Explore Spanish/English borrowings.** English has borrowed many words from Spanish, Spanish has borrowed from English, and both have borrowed from French. In this activity students look over a list of Spanish words with English cognates (Slide 3.46) and decide on the most likely origin for each word. The class then compares their answers to the correct answers in Slide 3.47 or 3.48.

    Students should try to rely on cultural knowledge and word forms instead of guessing. For instance, Spanish borrowed from English the technical terms *robot* and *video*, and also three words whose irregular stress might set off alarm bells: *champú*, *suéter*, and *fútbol*. However, the goal of the activity is not to get every answer right, but rather for students to think about the cross-cultural currents that have affected both languages.

*Take-home project*

- **Identify new-ish Spanish words.** A Google search for "palabras nuevas" will find articles about words recently added to the Real Academia Española's dictionary. In this activity, students work at home to create a master list of such words, sharing it in the cloud to avoid duplicates, perhaps in a spreadsheet modeled on the table shown in Slide 3.49. The class should decide ahead of time how many words each student should aim to find. As a follow-up, students might analyze the resulting list. For example, which semantic domains (such as technology) do these words pertain to? Which languages are they borrowed from? Where do non-borrowed words come from? Students might also vote for their favorite word(s), explaining their choices, or write paragraphs or dialogues using as many new words as possible.

    Another possible search term for this activity is "palabra del año Fundéu." Fundéu is a Spanish non-profit linked to the RAE that since 2013 has designated an annual "palabra del año" and eleven runners-up. Most *palabras del año* have been new words, although Fundéu has also selected some existing words that have acquired recent prominence (*refugiado*, 2015), perhaps with some change of meaning or affect (*populismo*, 2016). The essays that accompany the annual announcement are always worth reading.

## Internal history

### The sound changes that shaped Spanish words

*Just the facts*

Just as the experiences of a lifetime inevitably transform a person's appearance, so too, centuries of active use transformed the core vocabulary of Spanish as it evolved from Latin. *Molliare* became *mojar, ferrus* became *hierro, numquam* became *nunca*, and on and on. These transformations were the result of several small changes that took place gradually but that combined to bring about dramatic results. Specifically, speakers dropped some sounds, modified others in certain contexts, and sometimes added sounds, all in the pursuit of rapid and comfortable speech (Hochberg 2016, 40–41). These types of changes are not unique to Spanish: consider, for example, the English speaker who drops the *t* of *right*, modifies the *ty* of *don't you* to a *ch*, or adds a syllable to pronounce *athlete* as *athalete*.

Slide 3.50 summarizes some of the most common *pérdidas, adiciones*, and *modificaciones* that took place as Latin words became Spanish. It also lists Latin sounds that were lost globally in Spanish, such as long vowels, and new sounds that Spanish added, such as the *ñ*. Slide 3.51 presents the same changes but adds a two-character code to each: P1–P6 for the *pérdidas*, A1–A3 for the *adiciones*, and M1–M4 for the *modificaciones*.

Besides the activities below, other activities later in the chapter ("Identifying doublets" and "Brainstorming descendants of *ille*") and the section "Drastic changes in the Latin noun system" offer a further opportunity for students to engage with these sound changes.

As Old Spanish developed into modern Spanish, another round of phonological changes simplified its set of sibilant consonants such as *s*. Besides *ch*, which was stable during this time period, Old Spanish had six sibilants, all produced with the tongue making light contact with the roof of the mouth. As shown in Slide 3.52, there were three points of contact, all fairly close to each other: the back of the upper front teeth (for *ts* and *dz*), the alveolar ridge behind the upper front teeth (for *s* and *z*), and the soft palate midway back in the mouth (for *sh* and the /ʒ/ of *pleasure*). This proliferation of closely related sounds may have caused confusion, especially during rapid conversations. In the sixteenth century, speakers simplified matters by merging the voiced consonants *dz*, *z*, and /ʒ/ with their voiceless counterparts *ts*, *s*, and *sh*; subsequently, the remaining sibilants were made more distinctive by moving *sh* back to create the sound /x/ (as in *ajo*) and, in Castile, moving the *ts* forward to create *th*. Outside of Castile, *ts* merged with *s*.

This transition thus explains three features of Spanish phonology that are of particular interest to English speakers: the lack of a *z* sound (which English has), the presence of /x/ (which English lacks), and the Castilian *th*, an unusual sound that both languages happen to have (see Chapter 1). For more details, including the quirky spelling changes that accompanied these developments, see Penny (2002, 98–103) and Pharies (2007, 152–54).

### Teacher talk

"Las palabras del latín se convirtieron en las palabras del español por un proceso largo y lento. Esta conversión fue el resultado de múltiples cambios pequeños. Para hacer más fácil el habla rápida, se eliminaron ciertos sonidos, se añadieron otros y se modificaron otros según su contexto. El español también eliminó varios sonidos latinos, como sus vocales largas, y añadió sonidos nuevos propios, como la *eñe* y la *che*."

### In-class activities

*   **Trace changes in words.** In this activity, students trace the evolution of a set of Spanish words from their Latin ancestors (Slide 3.53; the color-coding in the slide is for formatting purposes only). The goal is to relate each step in each word's development to one of the specific changes shown in Slide 3.51. The teacher should therefore display Slide 3.51 and distribute copies of Slide 3.53, so that the students can label each step in the words' evolutions with the relevant two-character code from Slide 3.51. For example, the change from *plōrāre* to *llorar* involved three steps: the loss of the long Latin vowels (P5) to create *plorare*, the change of *pl* to *ll* (A3) to create *llorare*, and finally the loss of final *e* (P1) to create *llorar*.

    One click on Slide 3.53 reveals the answers for *llorar* (P5, A3, P1) so that this word can serve as a model; a second click reveals the other answers.
*   **Preview Spanish in the Appendix Probi.** Slide 3.28 included a fragment of the Appendix Probi (an early pedagogical text) as an example of the kinds of evidence linguists draw on to learn about Vulgar Latin. The full Appendix Probi listed a few hundred rules for avoiding errors common at the time. These "errors" are of interest because they represent changes in Vulgar Latin that would pave the way for Spanish and other Romance languages. Each rule had the form "X not Y."

    In this activity students relate eighteen rules from the Appendix Probi to the modern Spanish words that descended from their Vulgar Latin "Y" forms (Slide 3.54). As in the previous activity, the simplest way to organize this activity is for students to annotate a copy of the slide. *Autoridad* and *pájaro* are already filled in as examples, and a click will display the remaining modern words.

    As a second step, students can identify the various sound changes listed in Slide 3.51 that applied to create the modern words. Two more clicks on Slide 3.54 will first set up this step, then display the relevant sound change codes.

Two final clicks highlight two additional historical Spanish processes reflected in the Appendix Probi. First, some diminutives became standard words, losing their diminutive sense; this is seen in *oricla* > *oreja*. (A recent example of the same process is *mantequilla*, originally a diminutive of *manteca*.) Second, *-a* and *-o* became the standard feminine and masculine endings, as seen in *socrus* > *suegra*, *neptis* > *nieta*, and *passer* > *pájaro*, replacing Latin's large variety of masculine and feminine endings. See also "Drastic changes in the Latin noun system" later in this chapter.

## Sources of Spanish words

### Just the facts

Most Spanish words come from Latin. Of these, about half passed directly into Spanish from Vulgar Latin (Hochberg 2016, 140); these form the core vocabulary of Spanish, and are its most frequent words. In fact, of the one hundred most frequent Spanish words (Davies 2006), only one is not from Vulgar Latin: *hasta*, which Spanish borrowed from Arabic. A second infusion of Latin began in the Middle Ages when priests, doctors, and other educated Spaniards began to incorporate Latin words into their speech and writing, from where it "trickled down" to the general population. In many cases, these newer words still co-exist with older words from the same Latin root: for example, older *bicha* and newer *bestia*, both from Latin *bestia*. Slide 3.55 presents several examples of such "doublets." The newer words are generally closer to the Latin roots in both form and meaning since they have had less time to evolve and diverge.

As discussed in the first part of this chapter, other tranches of Spanish vocabulary reflect the different phases of Spanish history. Thus Spanish borrowed vocabulary from pre-Roman languages, from Visigothic and other Germanic languages, from Arabic, from the indigenous languages of Latin America, and, in modern times, from French and English. In addition, Spanish has borrowed significant amounts of vocabulary from other Romance languages and from Greek, among other languages. Each of these sources tends to be associated with certain semantic domains: science for Greek, food for French, music for Italian, technology for English, and so on. In some cases words from different sources can be recognized by their form, such as Arabic nouns that begin with *al-* (recall Slide 3.35) and Greek nouns that end with *-ma*, many of which are masculine in Spanish.

Regardless of their source, most borrowed words are nouns. This is a frequent pattern in other cases of language contact worldwide.

### Teacher talk

"La mayoría del vocabulario español viene del latín. Muchas palabras latinas originaron en el latín hablado por los soldados y colonizadores romanos que habitaban la península ibérica durante el Imperio Romano. Estas todavía son las palabras más frecuentes en el español de hoy. Otras palabras latinas entraron en el idioma más recientemente. El español también ha absorbido vocabulario de muchos otros idiomas, incluso los idiomas prerromanos de la península ibérica, el visigodo y otros idiomas germánicos, el árabe, los idiomas indígenas de Latinoamérica, el griego, los otros idiomas romances (sobre todo el francés) y el inglés."

*In-class activities*

- **Rank the sources of Spanish words.** Where do Spanish words come from? In this activity students estimate the relative contribution of various languages to the Spanish lexicon. The candidate languages are shown in Slide 3.56, along with three categories to place them into: the most important language (this will be Latin), other important languages (Arabic, French, and Greek), and less important languages. Clicking on the slide reveals these answers. A further click shows that other sizable chunks of Spanish vocabulary were apparently invented by Spanish speakers or are of unknown origin.

  Students might be surprised to learn that more Spanish words come from French than from Portuguese and Catalan, which are linguistically closer. An explanation lies in the leading role that France has played in religion, science, and the arts as well as the close historical connection (in both war and peace) between Spain and France.

- **Identify doublets.** As described above, "doublets" are pairs of Spanish words that come from the same Latin root, where one descended from Vulgar Latin and the other is a more recent borrowing (Slide 3.55). Slide 3.57 focuses on a set of doublets whose older members (the ones from Vulgar Latin) are common words. In this activity, students try to deduce these words; *leal* is filled in as an example. A click reveals the correct answers.

  The teacher can link this activity with the previous topic on sound changes from Latin to Spanish. This activity could introduce that topic, with students comparing the older Spanish words in Slide 3.57 to their Latin roots and identifying patterns of change. Or it could be a follow-up or review activity, giving students another chance to identify examples of the sound changes in Slide 3.50 or 3.51.

- **Match borrowed words with their sources.** This activity acquaints students with the variety of languages besides Latin that have contributed vocabulary to Spanish. Students attempt to match the words in Slide 3.58 with the source languages shown in the middle of the slide. Wherever possible, students should rely on general cultural knowledge (e.g. many operas are Italian) and common word patterns (e.g. Arabic words beginning with *-al*, Greek words ending with *-ma*) rather than guessing. A click on the slide reveals the words' actual origins.

- **Predict the origins of borrowed words.** This is a more challenging version of the previous activity. It replaces Slide 3.58 with Slide 3.59, which lacks the list of candidate source languages. Again, a click on the slide reveals the word origins.

- **Find semantic patterns in borrowed words.** Borrowed words in Spanish tend to fall into different semantic categories depending on their language of origin. Activities in the earlier part of this chapter explored borrowings from pre-Roman languages, Arabic, and Germanic languages. This activity takes up borrowings from Greek and English, two lingua francas of the ancient world and today, and from Romance languages other than Spanish: French and Occitan (a language of southern France), Portuguese and Galician (the ancestral source of Portuguese), and Italian. Students examine words from each language (Slides 3.60 and 3.61) and decide on the categories that best fit each group.

  There are no "right" answers for this activity, but some categories should stand out:

  - Greek: arts, religion, science, and social structure. The most unusual word on this list is the abstract adjective *cada*. (As mentioned earlier in this section, most borrowed words are nouns.)
  - English: commerce, fashion, media, science/technology, and sports.
  - French and Occitan: religion, nature, military, house, government, food, courtly life, and clothing. The semantic breadth of these borrowings reflects the intimate historical ties between Spain and France.
  - Portuguese and Galician: seafaring.
  - Italian: the arts (theater, music, visual arts, architecture), finance, maritime and military, and food and drink.

*Take-home projects*

- **Research the origins of words from a semantic domain.** In this activity and the next, students use the online dictionary of the Real Academia Española (rae.es) to look up the etymologies of different sets of words. This gives students the chance to see the roots of Spanish for themselves.

  In this first activity, each student, or pair of students, looks up the origins of words from a different semantic domain, such as clothing terms, body parts, fruits, kitchen items, technology, chemistry, and so on. Teachers can distribute lists of words to look up, or students can create their own, of a specified length (perhaps twenty words). Each student should first take notes on their individual words' origins, then create a table to summarize their results. In class, students can combine their summary tables to create one master table, with one column per source language and one row per semantic domain. The source languages that dominate Spanish vocabulary will quickly become clear, and likewise, to some extent, their relative importance in the different domains. It may be interesting for the class (or individual students) to predict the overall and domain-specific rankings ahead of time, then compare these predictions with reality.

Slide 3.62 shows an example of such an analysis of fourteen clothing terms, for which Latin and French turn out to be the two dominant sources. In this analysis the "other" category includes words that either lack an etymology in the Real Academia dictionary, such as *calcetín*, or that have a non-standard origin, such as *corbata*, which is a coinage based on a nationality (Croatian). The class should decide ahead of time whether to classify words that passed through another language en route to Spanish, such as *camisa/camiseta* and *chaleco*, according to the language from which Spanish borrowed them (Latin and Italian), as in Slide 3.62, or their original language (Celtic and Turkish).

- **Research the origins of words in a text.** In this activity, students, or pairs of students, use the Real Academia Española dictionary (rae.es) to look up the origins of all the words in a short text. For greatest interest, each student should analyze a different text, such as the first fifty words of a newspaper article of their own choosing, or the beginnings of different chapters of a book they are reading. As in the previous activity, students should first take notes on their words, then summarize the results, with the summaries then combined in class, with one row per text and one column per source language. Each column can then be summed, with the column totals serving as an estimate of the distribution of word origins in Spanish.

  The class must decide ahead of time whether they will count **words** or **word uses**. Since the most frequently used words are overwhelmingly from Latin, this language will inevitably swamp an analysis based on word uses. For example, there are likely to be many uses of *ser*, many of *el/la/los/las*, and so on. Slide 3.63 illustrates both approaches for an analysis of the first fifty words in *Don Quijote*, with word uses counted on the left and words counted on the right.

- **Greek or not Greek?** In this activity, students explore the origin and gender of Spanish words that end with -*ma*. Slide 3.64 contains instructions for the activity, Slide 3.65 lists a set of words to look up, and Slide 3.66 uses color-coding and animation to present the answers to the first three questions in the instructions. A series of clicks on Slide 3.64 will display answers to the *preguntas de interpretación*.

### Changes in meaning

*Just the facts*

An earlier section traced common changes in the form (pronunciation) of Spanish words over time. In many cases meanings changed as well, following patterns of semantic change seen also in other languages. For example, a *villano* was downgraded from a peasant to a villain, as in English, while a *caballo* was upgraded from a nag to a horse. (An example of an upgrade in English is the slangy use of *bad* or *sick* as a compliment.) Slide 3.67 shows these and other examples of some common types of semantic change as seen in Spanish.

### Teacher talk

"A través de los años, el sentido de muchas palabras ha cambiado. Por ejemplo, *caballo* originalmente quería decir un caballo viejo o de mala salud, mientras que un *villano* era un paisano, no una persona mala."

### In-class activity

• **Categorize changes in meaning.** In this activity students try to place each change in meaning shown in Slide 3.68 into one of the categories shown in Slide 3.67. The correct categories are color-coded in Slide 3.69.

## Por and para

### Just the facts

Mastering the difference between *por* and *para* is challenging for Spanish students, mostly because the two words have so many different meanings. Like first-language Spanish learners, students usually acquire these meanings one at a time (see Chapter 5). Knowing the historical relationship between *por* and *para* can be helpful during this process, and also useful when trying to express 'for' in an unfamiliar context.

As shown in Slide 3.70, *para* originated in Old Spanish when speakers began adding *a* to *por* to create prepositional meanings with a directional flavor. *Pora* eventually changed to *para*, but the directional generalization stayed. Consider, for example, the basic uses of *para* shown in Slide 3.71. The deadline of *mañana* is a temporal destination of the *tarea*, the *regalo* ends up with its recipient, the *tren* goes to Madrid, and so on.

### Teacher talk

"La palabra *para* originó en el antiguo español cuando los hablantes combinaron las dos preposiciones *por* y *a*. Luego *pora* se convirtió en *para*. Es por eso que muchos significados de *para* tienen un aspecto direccional."

### In-class activity

• **Identify directional aspects of *para* uses.** In this activity students try to identify a directional aspect of as many basic uses of *para* as possible. Teachers may use the list of uses in Slide 3.71 or their own. Groups of students may simply discuss the different uses and try to identify their directional aspects (if any). Another approach is for students to illustrate an example of each usage in a way that incorporates a directional arrow.

### The many descendants of Latin ille 'that'

*Just the facts*

Remarkably, Latin had neither definite articles nor third-person pronouns. By the time of Old Spanish, these had evolved from the various forms of the Latin demonstrative *ille*, the Latin equivalent of Spanish *aquel*. As shown with a series of clicks on Slide 3.72, the several forms of *ille* gave rise to the subject pronouns *él*, *ella*, *ellos*, and *ellas*, the direct and indirect object pronouns *lo(s)*, *la(s)*, and *le(s)*, and neuter *ello* and *lo*. This is a remarkable case of linguistic productivity.

Latin *ille* also survives, in mutated form, with its original demonstrative meaning: after Vulgar Latin added *accu* 'behold' to it as a prefix, *accu-ille* evolved into *aquel*.

*Teacher talk*

"Muchas de las palabras más comunes del español vienen de las varias formas de una sola palabra latina: el demostrativo *ille*, que tenía el mismo significado que *aquel* en español. *Ille* es la fuente de los artículos definidos *el*, *la*, *los* y *las*, y de todos los pronombres españoles de tercera persona: sujeto, complemento directo y complemento indirecto. Es interesante que aunque el latín no tenía estas palabras, esta falta no impedía nada la capacidad expresiva del idioma."

*In-class activity*

• **Brainstorm descendants of *ille*.** In this activity students try to predict which Spanish words are descended from the various forms of *ille*. The teacher should show Slide 3.72 (without clicking on it) and explain that the demonstrative *ille* is the source of sixteen important function words in Spanish. Students should work together to try to figure out what these words are. Writing a list of the Spanish words is sufficient. The teacher can then click on the slide to identify the Spanish words and the specific forms of *ille* they came from. This is a good time to make the point that Latin got along for centuries without these words, which are so vital to Spanish. How is that possible?

  If the class has already studied "the sound changes that shaped Spanish words" (Slide 3.50, this activity offers an opportunity to review and reinforce this topic. Students can observe the change of *u* to *o* (*illum* and *illud* > *lo*) and *i* to *e* (*illi* and *illis* > *le* and *les*, *illud* > *ello*), the loss of the final consonants -*d* and -*m* and the final vowel -*e* (*ille* > *el* and *él*), and the elimination of the contrast between long and short vowels. Not apparent from the spelling, but still significant, was the change of the long Latin *ll* to the Spanish *ll* sound in *ello(s)* and *ella(s)*.

## The evolution of the Spanish verb system

### Just the facts

As Latin evolved into Spanish its system of verb conjugations changed profoundly. In fact, only three Latin conjugations survive in Spanish with their original meaning: the present and imperfect indicative and the present subjunctive.

As shown with three initial clicks on Slide 3.73, several Latin conjugations were lost completely: all the passive conjugations, and four active conjugations as well (two future and two past). Two more clicks show that three of the remaining Latin conjugations took on new functions in Spanish: the Latin perfect became the Spanish preterite (a different "flavor" of past tense), and the two Latin pluperfects – indicative and subjunctive – evolved into the Spanish -*ra* and -*se* imperfect subjunctives. Two final clicks highlight the surviving three Latin tenses, and also the creation of several new Spanish conjugations based on the verb *haber*. These include the future and conditional, in which *haber*-based endings were attached to the infinitive (Slide 3.74), as well as the many compound perfects (present perfect, pluperfect, and so on), both indicative and subjunctive.

In fact, the evolution of the Spanish future tense nicely illustrates the cyclic nature of grammatical development: over and over, new forms have arisen out of independent words, replacing older forms that arose the same way (Slide 3.75). Looking furthest back in time, the endings of the original Latin future indicative came from the proto-Indo-European verb root *\*bhuH*- 'to become.' The Latin future was replaced by the Spanish future conjugation, whose endings come from *haber*. Today, a new Spanish future, based on the verb *ir*, competes robustly with the Spanish conjugated future, and is in the process of supplanting it in Latin America (see "Variation in verb use" in Chapter 4).

### Teacher talk

"Solo tres conjugaciones latinas sobreviven en el español con sus significados originales: el presente del indicativo y del subjuntivo, y el imperfecto indicativo. Muchas conjugaciones han desaparecido a través de los siglos. Unas sobrevivieron pero con significados nuevos. Finalmente, varias conjugaciones españolas son creaciones nuevas, todas basadas en el verbo *haber*."

### In-class activity

• **Match Spanish conjugations to Latin.** This activity dramatizes the losses, changes in meaning, and innovations that converted the Latin verb system into Spanish. Each student (or student pair) receives a copy of the two documents embedded in Slide 3.76, which summarize the Latin and Spanish verb systems. (The Spanish document does not list all the perfect conjugations, but only the present perfect and pluperfect indicatives.) The students should cut the Spanish document into ten pieces, one per conjugation, and attempt to place each Spanish conjugation on top of the Latin conjugation it evolved from, if any. The "leftover" Spanish conjugations will all be *haber*-based.

The teacher can jump-start this process by clicking on Slide 3.73 to show which Latin conjugations were lost. As students work, the teacher should also make sure that students do not mistakenly select the Latin future indicative as the source of the modern Spanish conjugated future (they look nothing alike), and should point out the changes in meaning of the Latin conjugations that led to the two Spanish imperfect subjunctives and the preterite (second click on Slide 3.73).

*Take-home project*

• **Trace the growth of the *ir a* future.** Students can use Google Books's Ngram Viewer to trace the growth over time of the *ir a* future at the expense of the conjugated future (http://books.google.com/ngrams; Michel et al. 2011). As an example, Slide 3.77 shows the changing frequencies of *vamos a comer* and *comeremos* between the years 1800 and 2000, with the *ir a* structure (in blue) overtaking the conjugated future (in red) in the late twentieth century. Each student can create a corresponding graph for a different pair of verb forms by typing them into the search bar, separated by a comma, and selecting "Spanish" for the corpus. Students can print the graphs and bring them to class for comparison or share them electronically.

As preparation for this activity, the class should decide on a list of comparisons to test and divide them among class members. The graphs are so easy to create that each student can do more than one comparison, if desired.

The Ngram Viewer is based on printed Spanish, and the increase in the *ir a* future is more marked in the spoken language. For this reason, not all graphs will show the *ir a* future overtaking the conjugated future as in Slide 3.77, but most should at least show a noticeable increase during the twentieth century.

### Irregular yo verbs (-zco and -go)

*Just the facts*

A little Spanish language history can go a long way toward explaining these two categories of irregular verbs.

The -*zco* ending of *conozco* and many other verbs simply preserves the form of their Latin roots: *conocer* comes from Latin *cognoscere*, *crecer* from *crescere*, *parecer* from *parescere*, etc. (Slide 3.78 and the more detailed 3.79). The original -*sc*- is preserved throughout the present subjunctive as well (*conozca*, *conozcas*, and so on). In all other forms of these verbs, including the infinitive, the -*e* or -*i* that followed the -*sc*- had a corrosive, softening effect on the consonant sequence, turning it into a simple *c* (pronounced *th* or *s*). The same historical pattern can be seen in other Spanish words: for example, while Latin *musca* 'fly' kept its -*sc*- as it evolved into Spanish *mosca*, *piscis* 'fish' softened into *peces* (Penny 2002, 180).

Once the -*zco* pattern was established, it spread to three other groups of Spanish verbs (Slide 3.79). The first group was verbs whose Latin roots did not have the -*scere* ending: for example, *ofrecer* (from Latin *offerre*) and *pertenecer* (from *pertinere*). The second group was newer -*cer* verbs created from Spanish adjectives and nouns, such as *enloquecer* (from *loco*) and *favorecer* (from *favor*). For the final group, the -*zco* pattern spread to verbs ending in -*ucir*, such as *lucir* and *reducir*. As a result of these tendencies almost all modern Spanish -*cer* verbs, and all -*ucir* verbs, ended up as -*zco* verbs. The only -*cer* exceptions are *hacer, cocer, ejercer, mecer, torcer, yacer*, and *vencer*, and compounds based on these verbs, such as *deshacer* and *retorcer*.

The -*go* ending of *hago* and many other verbs reflects a broader change from Latin *k* (spelled *c*) to Spanish *g* between vowels, where the second vowel was *a*, *o*, or *u* (Slide 3.80). For example, Latin *securus* and *formica* became Spanish *seguro* and *hormiga*. The -*go* endings first appeared in the frequent verbs *decir* and *hacer*, whose first person singular Latin forms were *dico* and *faco* (originally *facio*, but the *i* was lost). Latin *k* likewise changed to *g* before *a* in the present subjunctive forms of these verbs, such as *diga* and *hagamos*. The new -*go* ending then spread to unrelated verbs such as *tener, venir, salir*, and *poner*. In other forms of *decir* and *hacer*, including the infinitive, the Latin *k* sound softened to a *th* or *s*, as was normal before *e* or *i* (e.g. Lat. *luce* > *luz* and *vicino* > *vecino*).

### Teacher talk

"La forma *conozco* refleja la forma original del verbo *conocer* en latín: *cognoscere*. Los verbos de tipo -*go*, como *hago*, son el resultado del mismo cambio que convirtió, por ejemplo, *aqua* a *agua*."

### Take-home project

- **Identify original -*zco* verbs.** The Spanish -*zco* verbs are a perfect illustration of the linguistic principal of analogy, whereby a pattern spreads between similar words. An example in English is the change of *weared* (the original past tense of *wear*) to *wore*, in analogy to verbs like *bear/bore* and *tear/tore*. As noted above, the -*zco* pattern started with a set of Latin verbs that ended in -*scere*, such as *cognoscere* and *parescere*, then spread to almost all Spanish verbs ending in -*cer*, and to all verbs ending in -*ucir*.

This activity gives students the chance to witness analogy first-hand by looking up the etymologies of a set of -*zco* verbs in the online dictionary of the Real Academia Española (rae.es). Some of these come from -*scere* verbs; most do not. The verbs and their origins are listed in Slides 3.81 and 3.82, respectively.

A class discussion after this activity can focus on the question of how a pattern like -*zco* actually spreads from word to word: that is, the mechanism of analogy. Do students think these changes start with incomplete learning by children, who naturally apply patterns as widely as possible (e.g. *falled* for *fell, mouses* for *mice*), or do they arise from adult speech, either in error or deliberately? How many speakers have to adopt an analogical form before it "counts" as normal Spanish? Do students believe that the remaining -*cer* "holdouts" listed above (e.g. *hacer* and *cocer*) are likely to adopt the -*zco* pattern in the future? Which verbs are most or least likely to change?

### Stem-changing verbs

#### Just the facts

Like -*zco* and -*go* verbs, stem-changing verbs have a straightforward historical explanation (Slide 3.83). Most verbs with the *e/ie* or *o/ue* alternation, such as *perder* and *poder*, come from Latin verbs whose stem vowel was a short *e* or *o*, sometimes written *ĕ* and *ŏ*, as in *pĕrdere* and *pŏtere*. In stressed syllables, these Latin short vowels became Spanish diphthongs (two-vowel sequences). (The same change is seen in words that are not verbs, such as *fiesta* and *puerta*, from Latin *fĕsta* and *pŏrta*.) The role of stress explains the characteristic "boot" pattern of stem-changing verbs, since stress in *nosotros* and *vosotros* forms falls on the verb ending instead of the stem. Verbs with an *e* or *o* stem vowel that does not change, such as *deber* and *poner*, generally had a long *ē* or *ō* in Latin.

Because the distinction between long and short vowels has been lost in Spanish, memorization is now the only way to know whether a verb with an *e* or *o* stem vowel has a stem change. In addition, some verbs that originally had a short vowel have acquired the stem change, while some that had a short vowel have become regular. *Entregar* (from *intĕgrare*) is an example of the former outcome, and *pensar* (from *pēnsare*) of the latter. This means that even Spanish students who know Latin have to memorize which verbs have the stem change today.

*Teacher talk*

"El latín diferenciaba entre vocales cortas y largas. Las vocales cortas *ĕ* y *ŏ* cambiaron a *ie* y *ue* cuando estaban en sílabas estresadas: por ejemplo, *fĕsta* y *pŏrta* en latín se convirtieron en *fiesta* y *puerta* en español. Los verbos con estas vocales sufrieron este cambio solo en las formas de la 'bota', donde ocurren en una sílaba estresada."

*In-class activities*

- **Look for differences between stem-changing and regular verbs.** Why does *costar* have a stem change but not *comprar*? This activity drives home the fact that stem-changing and regular verbs are indistinguishable in modern Spanish. Students work in pairs or groups to try to find differences between common verbs of both types (Slide 3.84). In fact there are none, for the historical reasons described above. This activity should therefore be kept to two or three minutes at the most to minimize frustration. Afterward, the teacher can show Slide 3.83 to explain the historical origin of the stem change.
- **Categorize stem-changing verbs.** Conjugating stem-changing verbs requires a minor feat of mental gymnastics: the speaker must simultaneously control both the stem alternation and the verb endings. This activity highlights the importance of developing this skill, while reinforcing basic knowledge of the distribution of these verbs. Slide 3.85 lists the fifty-one stem-changing verbs that are among the one thousand most frequent Spanish verbs (Davies 2006). Students work in pairs or groups to divide the verbs into categories based on their stem change and conjugation class, organizing them into a table such as the one also shown on the slide.

  The results, as shown in Slide 3.86, will draw students' attention to the existence of *elie* and *olue* verbs in all three conjugation classes. In addition, students will observe other distributional facts: that the *eli* alternation is limited to *-ir* verbs, that *jugar* is the only *ulue* verb, and that *dormir* and *morir* are the only *-ir* verbs (in all of Spanish!) with an *olue* alternation. For an explanation of these oddities, see Hochberg 2016, 238–41.

## The extreme irregularity of ser and ir

*Just the facts*

*Ser* and *ir* are the most irregular Spanish verbs. While some forms of *ser* are clearly related to the infinitive, such as *siendo* and *sed*, forms like *era* and *fue* appear to have come out of nowhere. Similarly, *ir* combines clearly related forms such as *ido* and *id* with out-of-nowhere forms like *vas* and, again, *fue*.

This complex picture arose because each of these verbs combined three distinct roots. *Ser* (Slide 3.87) merged the Latin verb *sedere* 'to sit' with *esse* 'to be,' which itself had merged two Proto-Indo-European roots meaning 'to be' and 'to become.' *Ir* (Slide 3.88) merged the Latin verbs *ire* 'to go,' *vadere* 'to go, to walk,' and *esse* 'to be.' The admixture of *esse* forms into *ir* explains why *ir* and *ser* have the same preterite and imperfect subjunctive conjunctions.

*Ser* and *ir* thus illustrate to an extreme degree the maxim explored in Chapter 2, that frequent verbs are most likely to be irregular. In fact, students may be interested to learn that the history of the English verb 'to be' is remarkably parallel to that of *ser* (Slide 3.89). Like Spanish, it is a combination of three verb roots. As in Spanish, two of these roots are the Proto-Indo-European verbs meaning 'to be' and 'to become.' And again as in Spanish, the third root, like Latin *sedere*, is a physical verb with a locational flavor: Proto-Indo-European root *$h_2$wes- 'to live, dwell, remain.'

### Teacher talk

"Los verbos *ser* e *ir* son los más irregulares del español porque cada uno es una combinación de tres verbos históricos. Es por eso que las formas diferentes de los verbos son tan distintas. Por ejemplo, unas formas del verbo *ser* vienen del verbo latino *sedere*, que quería decir 'sentarse', y las formas de *ir* que empiezan con *uve*, como *voy* y *vaya*, vienen del verbo latino *vadere*, que quería decir 'andar'. Las formas de *ir* que empiezan con *efe*, como *fue* y *fuera*, vienen de *ser*."

### In-class activity

- **Discover the multiple sources of *ser* and *ir*.** In this activity, students analyze the conjugation charts of the verbs *ser* and *ir*, grouping together similar-looking conjugations within each verb. For example, *ir*'s present indicative and present subjunctive are clearly related because all the forms begin with *v*. For this activity, each student (or pair of students) needs a copy of the conjugation charts embedded in Slide 3.90. The students (or the teacher, ahead of time) should cut each chart into its component conjugations. After the students have grouped the conjugations as best as they can, the teacher can show Slides 3.87 and 3.88 to explain the verbs' origins and Slide 3.89 for a comparison with English.

  The groupings for *ir* are straightforward, since all forms begin with either *i/y*, *v*, or *f*. When showing Slide 3.88, the instructor should point out the interesting split in the imperatives (*id* from *ire* and *ve* from *vadere*) and the importation of the preterite and the imperfect subjunctive from *ser*. With *ser* the present indicative will be a sticking point, since some of its forms begin with *e* and some with *s*. The teacher can explain that this conjugation, which arose from the single Proto-Indo-European root *$h_1es$, was already highly irregular in Latin.

## Drastic changes in the Latin noun system

### Just the facts

Spanish eliminated two key aspects of Latin's complicated noun system (Slide 3.91). The first was its "case" endings, such as -*a* and -*am*, which appeared on nouns, adjectives, and pronouns and indicated their role in a sentence, such as subject or object. (For example, the Latin sentences meaning 'Boy loves girl' and 'Girl loves boy' in the slide have the same word order, but different word endings.) The second was Latin's neuter gender.

The result of these changes was the drastically simpler Spanish system, with only four basic noun endings based on three consistent markers (-*o*/-*a* for binary gender and -*s* for plural), compared to over a hundred noun endings in Latin.

As shown with a click on the slide, the Spanish noun endings -*o*, -*os*, -*a*, and -*as* derived from a small subset of the Latin accusative (direct object) endings. The change of the singular endings from -*um* and -*am* to -*o* and *a*, and the loss of the long vowels in plural -*ōs* and -*ās*, reflect normal patterns of sound change from Latin to Spanish (Slide 3.50).

### Teacher talk

"El sistema nominal en latín era mucho más complicado que nuestro sistema español. En latín los nombres, adjetivos y pronombres tenían terminaciones especiales que diferenciaban entre sujetos, objetos, y otros roles sintácticos. El español ya no las tiene. También, en latín había tres géneros: masculino, femenino y neutro. En español solo quedan masculino y femenino."

### In-class activity

•   **Consider the Latin case system and its disappearance.** The Latin case system represented in Slide 3.91 is so alien to speakers of English or Spanish that it can be hard to imagine people actually speaking such a language. Nevertheless, this system, inherited from Proto-Indo-European, flourished for centuries, and similar systems are found in many modern languages, both Indo-European and not (e.g. Russian and Hungarian). Speakers of such languages learn case endings the same way that one learns to conjugate verbs.

In this activity, students think about and discuss what it would be like to speak a language, like Latin, that has case endings. What kinds of errors might a child make when learning the language? Or a second language learner? A case system to some extent makes word order more flexible, as in the 'Boy loves girl' example pictured on Slide 3.91. What advantages could this have in writing (especially in poetry) or in speech?

Students can also survey the Latin system depicted on the slide and hypothesize why it changed so drastically as the language evolved into Spanish. Was it too complicated to survive? What role might have been played by the sound changes described earlier in this chapter (Slide 3.50)? (Hint: recall that many word-final sounds were lost.) Are simple patterns, like a single -o/-a contrast for gender, and a uniform -s ending, always easier to learn?

The following references are cited in this chapter's text and/or its accompanying PowerPoint presentation.

## References

Corominas, J. 1973. *Breve diccionario etimológico de la lengua castellana*. Madrid: Gredos.

Davies, M. 2006. *A frequency dictionary of Spanish*. Routledge Frequency Dictionaries. London: Routledge.

Eberhard, D. M., G. F. Simons, and D. D. Fennig, eds. 2020. *Ethnologue: Languages of the world*. 23rd ed. Dallas, TX: SIL International. Retrieved from http://www.ethnologue.com.

Fortson, B. W. IV. 2010. *Indo-European language and culture: An introduction*. Blackwell textbooks in linguistics. Chichester: John Wiley & Sons.

Hochberg, G. 2016. *¿Por qué? 101 questions about Spanish*. London: Bloomsbury.

Looney, D. and N. Lusin. 2019. Enrollments in languages other than English in United States Institutions of Higher Education, Summer 2016 and Fall 2016: Final Report. Modern Language Association. https://www.mla.org/content/download/110154/2406932/2016-Enrollments-Final-Report.pdf.

Michel, J-B., Y. K. Shen, A. P. Aiden, A. Veres, M. K. Gray, The Google Books Team, J. P. Pickett, et al. 2011. Quantitative analysis of culture using millions of digitized books. *Science* 331: 176–82.

Penny, R. 2002. *A history of the Spanish language*. 2nd ed. Cambridge: Cambridge University Press.

Pharies, D. A. 2007. *A brief history of the Spanish language*. Chicago, IL: University of Chicago Press.

Real Academia Española (RAE). 2019. *Diccionario de la lengua española*, versión 23.3. http://www.rae.es/rae.html.

Trask, R. L. 1997. *The history of Basque*. London: Routledge.

Vigo. 2009. Ethnic-linguistic map [of] Southwestern Europe. https://commons.wikimedia.org/wiki/File:Linguistic_map_Southwestern_Europe-en.gif.

Weinreich, M. 1945. YIVO and the problem of our time. *YIVO Bleter* 25: 3–18. http://download.hebrewbooks.org/downloadhandler.ashx?req=43629.

# Chapter 4

# How does Spanish vary?

Spanish is not monolithic. As with any other language, the language experience of different Spanish speakers varies depending on where they live and their socioeconomic status, age, and gender. Speakers also change their way of speaking depending on the context of a conversation. Slide 4.1 summarizes these factors and provides some examples.

The most important factor affecting variation in Spanish is geography. Accordingly, this chapter begins with an overview of Spanish dialects, both in Spain and in Latin America. Geography also determines what other languages a Spanish speaker interacts with, since every Hispanic country is multilingual to some degree. The dialect overview is therefore followed by a section on multilingualism: what other languages are spoken in Spanish-speaking countries, how this has in some cases affected the local varieties of Spanish, and how bilingual speakers move back and forth between languages ("code-switching").

Variation in Spanish affects every aspect of the language: its pronunciation, vocabulary, and grammar. The remainder of the chapter considers several topics in each of these areas, exploring their dialectal differences and/or sociological variation due to class, age, gender, and formality. Some examples are the weakening or loss of final -s (pronunciation), words like *tortilla*, whose meaning varies depending on one's dialect (vocabulary), and variation in the second person singular (grammar).

Besides its intrinsic interest, and its connection to Hispanic culture, variation is additionally worth studying because it can be a sign of ongoing change in Spanish, a concept first demonstrated by Labov (1963) for English. In some cases a variant form has emerged "from below" – in a non-prestigious form of the language – and is catching on with other speakers. This appears to be the case, for example, with the velar (guttural) *r* of Puerto Rico, which many speakers now adopt in formal as well as informal speech. In other instances a standard variant is asserting itself "from above" at the expense of a lower-prestige form. This appears to be happening, for example, in parts of Andalusia, where speakers are adopting either the usual Andalusian *seseo* or the Castilian *s/th* distinction in place of the local *ceceo* (pronunciation of *s* as *th*). Both these examples are described in more detail later in the chapter.

Some of the activities in this chapter simply **expose** students to different varieties of Spanish. Others give students the chance to **learn** more about a specific aspect of variation: for example, by researching the features of a particular dialect. Some encourage students to **experience** differences for themselves: for example, by attempting tongue-twisters with *seseo*, with *ceceo*, or Castilian style. And in others, students **explore** the real-world consequences of language variation, such as language politics in Spain or the problems faced by Latin American immigrants in the United States who speak neither English nor Spanish.

Spanish speakers are typically aware of variation in their language and often care deeply about it. The type of Spanish they speak is a vital expression of their Hispanic identity, and also affects how other speakers perceive them. Therefore, this chapter also includes several activities in which students **ask a native speaker** about dialectal features and their implications.

For a full list of the chapter's activities and projects, and their suitability for different levels of instruction, see Appendices A and B.

*Teacher talk*

"No hay una sola variedad del español. Hay múltiples dialectos del idioma en los varios países y regiones de habla española. Además el español varía según la clase social, la edad y el sexo del hablante, y las circunstancias de una conversación."

*In-class activity*

•   **Brainstorm about language variation.** As a warm-up for the general topic of variation in Spanish, groups of students brainstorm about the different factors that affect how people speak a language, using English as a familiar example. The class may conduct this activity as a competition to see which group can identify and exemplify the most factors (Slide 4.2). As shown there, the teacher can seed the discussion by listing *dialectos* or *geografía* as a first factor and eliciting examples of different English dialects and some of their features. Alternatively, the activity can be a more personal discussion based on students' experience with other English speakers and their own use of the language (Slide 4.3).

## Dialects and multilingualism

### Spanish dialects

*Just the facts*

Within Spain, language variation due to geography takes two forms. First, as discussed in the next section, standard Spanish, or *castellano*, is only one of the country's four principal languages. Second, Spanish itself has two primary dialects in Spain: northern and southern (Andalusian), which are culturally and linguistically dominated by Madrid and Seville, respectively. As shown in Slide 4.4, and illustrated in the videos linked to in Slide 4.5, the pronunciation and grammar of these two dialects differ significantly.

The characteristics of southern Spanish shown in Slide 4.4 all involve the simplification or loss of language features. Linguists agree that these changes are primarily a linguistic consequence of the Reconquista, the gradual takeover of Moorish-occupied southern Spain between 711 and 1492 (see "Reconquista" section in Chapter 3). During this period Castilian Spanish, the primary language of the northern forces, came into prolonged contact with the languages then spoken in the south: Mozarabic (the local Romance language) and Arabic. Sounds and grammatical features are commonly simplified or lost in such contact situations, in part because speakers of an incoming language attempt to make themselves understood by the local population, a process called "linguistic accommodation" (Penny 2000, 38–42).

Spain's primary Atlantic ports (Cadiz and Huelva) are in the south, so that most of the Spaniards who colonized Latin America came from this region (Penny 2002, 26). For this reason Latin American Spanish shares with Andalusian Spanish the characteristics shown in Slide 4.4.

Other aspects of European migration to Latin America have contributed to dialectal variation within this region. Areas that were in frequent contact with Spain kept up with ongoing changes in the language there, such as *tú* overtaking *vos* as the dominant second person singular subject pronoun. (For more details, see "Subject pronouns" later in this chapter.) In parts of Latin America that Spain only sparsely settled, indigenous languages remained robust, and have influenced the pronunciation and even grammar of the local varieties of Spanish. (For more details, see "Multilingualism in Latin America" later in this chapter.) Finally, large-scale Italian immigration in Argentina (and Uruguay) gave its Spanish an up-and-down intonation pattern that sounds distinctively Italian (Pharies 2007, 114).

These historical factors, along with the natural tendency of language to evolve, have given rise to a variety of distinctive Latin American dialects. Three that are particularly recognizable are Argentinian, Caribbean, and Andean Spanish; see Slide 4.6 for some characteristics of these dialects, and Slide 4.7 for links to videos of speakers of these dialects.

From a linguist's perspective, all dialects of Spanish are equally valid. But speakers of Spanish do not perceive all dialects equally. Castilian Spanish has historically enjoyed great prestige as the language of the Spanish crown and of the Real Academia Española. In modern times Latin American Spanish has gained increasing cultural prominence because of its larger number of speakers, its renowned literature, and official academic recognition. However, studies have shown that speakers of Spanish worldwide still look "most favorably" on Castilian Spanish, which they consider "proper"

(FMOHC 2018, 500–501). In this writer's experience, Spanish speakers generally consider Colombian Spanish superior to other Latin American dialects, and describe Caribbean, Chilean, and some varieties of Mexican Spanish as less prestigious and/or harder to understand.

Besides the activities described below, many activities later in this chapter address dialectal differences in specific language features, such as vocabulary or subject pronouns.

### Teacher talk

"No existe ninguna versión única del español; de hecho, el idioma tiene muchos dialectos. El español de España se divide más o menos entre el español del norte y del sur. El español del sur de España es la fuente del español de Latinoamérica por lo cual se parecen bastante. Además hay muchas variedades regionales en Latinoamérica, como los dialectos de Argentina, del Caribe y de los Andes. Los idiomas indígenas de Latinoamérica, y también el italiano hablado por millones de inmigrantes a Argentina, han influido unos dialectos latinoamericanos."

### In-class activities

- **Discuss dialects in general.** Students are already aware of variation in English dialects, from the Southern American drawl to the use of *hoagie, submarine, grinder,* or *hero* to describe the same kind of sandwich. In this activity students discuss dialectal variation in general and in English as a warm-up for learning about Spanish dialects. Slide 4.8 lists some possible discussion topics for the full class or smaller groups of students.
- **Listen to examples of different dialects.** Slides 4.5 and 4.7 contain links to videos of speakers of two dialects of Spanish in Spain and three in Latin America. The class listens to these videos and takes notes on what they hear. How intelligible is each dialect? Is it different from the Spanish in their textbook and/or their teacher's Spanish? If the class does this activity after reviewing the dialect characteristics in Slides 4.4 and 4.6, students can try to observe them in the videos.

### Take-home projects

- **Profile a dialect.** Each student, or group of students, chooses (or is assigned) a dialect of Spanish from the list in Slide 4.9. These can be subdivided; for example, Caribbean Spanish varies from country to country, and Mexican Spanish has central, northwestern, Yucatan, and coastal dialects (Pharies 2007, 227). Each student creates a profile of his or her assigned dialect that contains the information listed in Slide 4.10 in the form of a poster, slide presentation, or oral report that can be shared with the class.

The most challenging part of this project will be finding source materials that are accurate but not too technical. Wikipedia (in English or Spanish) is the easiest solution if the teacher allows it. Mackenzie (1999–2020) is a reliable English-language website with information on several dialects, both in Spain and Latin America. Finally, Lipski (1994), republished in Spanish in 1996, has detailed descriptions of several Latin American dialects. Lipski (2008) is more recent and somewhat more accessible but covers fewer dialects.

- **Profile a country's dialect(s).** This project is similar to the dialect profiles described just above, except that each student or group of students profiles the dialect(s) of Spanish spoken in a specific country. (This is different from the "Country language profiles" activity in Chapter 1, which focuses on language use in each country.) The profiles should include the information in Slide 4.11.
- **Learn from "dialectos del español" videos.** A YouTube search for "dialectos del español" or "acentos del español" will yield many videos that demonstrate a variety of dialects. Pairs or groups of students each choose one such video (it should be in Spanish) and take notes on the characteristics of three dialects represented in the video. It will probably be necessary to listen to the relevant parts of the video multiple times. Each group then plays those parts of their video for the class and comments on the dialectal aspects they observed.
- **Ask a native speaker about dialects.** This activity requires students to work with a native speaker partner as described in the Introduction. Each student should ask their partner about their own dialect of Spanish and/or other dialects. Slides 4.12 and 4.13 include sample questions, or the class can develop its own list. Students can summarize their findings in a written, oral, or graphic report.

## Multilingualism in Spain

### Just the facts

Standard Spanish is one of four languages native to Spain; just over eighty percent of the country's population speak it as a first language (Slide 4.14). The most widely spoken minority language of Spain is Catalan, found in the northeastern provinces of Catalonia, Valencia, and the Balearic Islands. It is closely related to the Occitan language of southern France. The second is Galician, found in the northwestern province of Galicia. It is similar to Portuguese, and in fact is the historic source of that language. Like standard Spanish, Catalan and Galician began as regional varieties of Vulgar Latin and blossomed into full-fledged languages with their own literature, press, schools, dictionaries, and language authorities. The smallest of Spain's minority languages is Basque (often called by its Basque name, *Euskera*), spoken in the northern provinces of the Basque Country and Navarra as well as southwestern France. It descends from Aquitanian, a language found in southwestern France at the time of the Roman Conquest, and is unrelated to any other known language.

Slide 4.15 shows a sample text in the three minority languages as well as Spanish, and Slide 4.16 links to videos of the languages. Basque is the clear outlier. Although it has absorbed a large amount of Spanish vocabulary over the centuries, its pronunciation, core vocabulary, and grammar remain completely alien to those of Spanish. On the other hand, while there are significant differences among Spanish, Catalan, and Galician, students should be able to recognize their overall similarity. In fact speakers of these three Romance languages can understand each other to a fair extent, as with Portuguese. For more detail, Slide 4.17 presents some striking differences between Spanish and Basque, and Slide 4.18 summarizes the main differences between Spanish and Catalan.

The Spanish constitution officially recognizes and protects Spain's minority languages (Slide 4.19). This is a dramatic change from the mid-twentieth century, when for four decades Francisco Franco's government designated Castilian Spanish as the only official language of Spain. Today language remains a controversial topic in Catalonia, where advocates of Catalan have promoted the language at the expense of Castilian, especially in schools. (See activity "Discuss the language controversy in Catalonian schools.") This language controversy is intimately connected to the region's separatist movement.

For more about Basque, see "Spain before Latin" in Chapter 3.

*Teacher talk*

"El español que estudiamos en esta clase es el primer idioma del 82% de los españoles. La mayoría de los demás hablan uno de tres idiomas: el catalán, el gallego y el vasco. El catalán y el gallego son lenguas romances que vienen del latín, como el español, mientras el vasco no está relacionado con ningún otro idioma conocido. Estos tres idiomas tienen estatus oficial como idiomas minoritarios en España, un estatus reconocido en la constitución del país. Sin embargo en Cataluña se encuentra hoy bastante conflicto entre el catalán y el castellano (sobre todo en las escuelas), una polémica relacionada con el movimiento separatista."

*In-class activities*

- **Map minority languages.** This activity can serve as a springboard for learning about Spain's minority languages and cultures. Working off Slide 4.20, or the more challenging Slide 4.21, groups of students tap into any existing knowledge they have of these languages to identify the regions of Spain where they are spoken. The teacher may choose to allow students to access the Internet if no group can complete this task. As a second step, each group should estimate the percentage of Spaniards for whom each of these languages is a first language. The teacher or a student can combine their estimates on the board and then show the correct numbers from Slide 4.14.

- **Listen to minority languages.** The teacher plays a minute or so of each video in Slide 4.16. For the Catalan and Galician segments, students should take and compare notes on how much they can understand, based on their knowledge of Spanish, and how the languages strike them. Galician is likely to be the easiest, and students may be able to understand a fair amount of Catalan. If they are familiar with other Romance languages, they may recognize the close relationship between Galician and Portuguese, and the overall sound of Catalan may remind them of Italian. For Basque, students may be able to recognize some Spanish words that the language has borrowed; everything else will be incomprehensible.

- **Read a Catalan text.** This activity gives students the chance to delve into Spain's most-spoken minority language. The teacher first identifies an interesting text, such as a recent article in the Catalan edition of *El País* (cat.elpais.com), and reads the first few paragraphs him/herself, with the help of automatic translation if necessary. In addition, the class should go over Slide 4.18 to become familiar with some differences between Spanish and Catalan.

  The teacher then adds line numbers to the chosen portion of the text and distributes it to the students, who attempt to read it (perhaps in pairs) by leveraging their knowledge of Spanish. As they do so, they should note examples of the characteristic Catalan features in Slide 4.18 such as the *va* past tense, *ç, l·l,* and the grave accent (*à, è, ò*). They should also take notes on obvious correspondences between the two languages (e.g. *oportunitat* ~ *oportunidad, com* ~ *como*) and underline words they cannot interpret.

  After completing a first pass the class should compare their notes on the text. This will yield examples of several characteristics of the language; additionally, working as a class, students should be able to reduce the common list of challenging words to a small set that the teacher can then interpret. As a final step, each pair of students may write out a full translation of the text into Spanish.

- **Discuss the language section of the Spanish Constitution.** Students read Article 3 of the Spanish Constitution (Slide 4.19) and discuss it in class. What are the practical consequences of this article? What aspects of life in Spain is it likely to affect? The United States Constitution does not mention languages. What cultural or historical differences between the two countries does this reflect?

- **Discuss the language controversy in Catalonian schools.** The *Ley de política lingüística* of the province (*Comunidad autónoma*) of Catalonia states that Catalan is the official language of instruction in the province, though schools must also teach Castilian Spanish as a second language (Slide 4.22). This law has been the subject of a slow-motion legal tug-of-war between provincial authorities and Castilian-speaking families who want their children educated in their own language. The central government has occasionally added fuel to the fire. Most notably, in the mid-2010s, the Mariano Rajoy government launched an initiative to *españolizar a los niños catalanes* by subsidizing private Castilian education in Catalonia as an alternative to the public Catalan schools, a move that sparked protests throughout the region (as seen in Slide 4.23) and eventually failed.

  The teacher can lead off a discussion of this topic by showing the text of the *Ley de política lingüística* (Slide 4.22) or a photograph of a pro-Catalan protest (Slide 4.23). The discussion can touch on issues such as local versus national control of education, the rights of minorities (here, Castilian speakers), and how the students would feel if they were growing up in Catalonia as members of a Castilian- or Catalan-speaking family. A class debate would be an appropriate way to explore the two sides of the controversy. For a deeper dive into this topic, the class can read and discuss one or more of the articles listed in Slide 4.24, or a more recent article that the teacher or a student identifies.

  The class can also compare the pro-Catalan educational policy of Catalonia (Slide 4.22) and the policies of Galicia and the Basque Country (Slide 4.25), which are more favorable to Castilian Spanish. Why are these so different?

*Take-home projects*

- **Profile a minority language.** Each student, or group of students, chooses (or is assigned) and researches a minority language of Spain. The core set of Catalan, Galician, and Basque can be supplemented by smaller languages such as Aragonese, Asturian, Berber (in Melilla), Llanito (in Gibraltar), Silbo Gomero (the whistling language of the Canary Islands), and Caló (the language of the Romani people). The profile should present the information in Slide 4.26 in the form of a poster, slide presentation, or oral report that students can share with the class.
- **Compare the Catalan/Castilian conflict to another language conflict.** Each student (or pair of students) chooses another language conflict somewhere in the world and compares it to the conflict between Catalan and Castilian Spanish in Catalonia. Some possibilities are bilingual education in the United States, French versus English in Quebec, and French

versus Flemish in Belgium. The result of this inquiry can be an oral report, a poster, a slide presentation, or a written essay.

*   **WebQuest: Explore advocacy groups.** Both sides of the Catalonian language controversy have advocacy groups: Somescola for supporters of Catalan education, and Convivencia cívica catalana for the Castilian minority. Each has a website (somescola.cat and convivenciacivicacatalana.org) that links to an active Twitter feed. In this WebQuest, the class researches and reports on the activities of these advocacy groups.

    Unless the class is too large, it should be divided in half, with each half assigned to each of the two advocacy groups. A student leader (or leadership team) of each group should assign specific published material from "their" advocacy group to each student. This might be a recent blog post or tweet, the "who we are" page of the group's website (*Qui som?* or *Presentación*), or a cartoon from Somescola's *Suports* page. Each student then reads their material, using translation software as needed to convert text into Castilian Spanish, and summarizes it as part of a table in a shared document, such as a Google Doc, as shown in Slide 4.27. Each half of the class can also prepare a group presentation that explains "their" advocacy group's perspective and activities. Or the two sides can have a debate that draws explicitly on each group's published material.

    If the class is too large, more than one student group can research each advocacy group.

*   **What's new with minority languages?** In this activity, each student reads and summarizes (orally or in writing) a recent news article about a minority language of Spain. So that each student reads a different article, the teacher can assign articles, or students can sign up for them in a shared document. The links in Slide 4.28 will help to locate possible articles.

### Multilingualism in Latin America

*Just the facts*

Latin America is a dramatically multilingual region by any measure. Tens of millions of Latin Americans speak hundreds of indigenous languages that belong to dozens of different language families (Slide 4.29, based on Hochberg 2016, 26). This is remarkably different from the language situation in Europe, where the expansion of Indo-European eliminated all but a handful of other language families (Chapter 3).

Latin America's indigenous languages have survived primarily in areas whose geography reduced their appeal to the Spanish *conquistadores* (Slide 4.30). Bolivia and Paraguay, the countries with today's most robust indigenous language presence, are Latin America's only land-locked countries, while Peru (and Guatemala), in the next tier, are mountainous (and jungled). At the other extreme, linguists estimate that in the Caribbean, which served as the Spanish gateway to the New World, the native Arahuacans (Arawaks) and their languages, such as Taino, died out within a few decades of Columbus's arrival (Whitehead 1999, 864).

The maps and the table in Slides 4.31 and 4.32 detail the indigenous languages that have the most native speakers today, and Slide 4.33 links to videos of people speaking some of them. For the most part these languages are spoken in southern Mexico and Guatemala, along the spine of the Andes, and in the heart of the South American interior. Most belong to the Quechuan, Otomanguean, and Mayan language families, which are specific to Latin America. Nahuatl is part of the Uto-Aztecan language family, which extends northward into the United States and includes Ute, Hopi, Shoshone, and Comanche, among other languages.

In regions of Latin America where these languages are most vibrant, bilingualism has been the norm for multiple generations, so that indigenous language features have affected the pronunciation and even grammar of the local varieties of Spanish. Slides 4.34 and 4.35 illustrate some such features of Mayan and Quechuan pronunciation, and of Guaraní grammar, respectively. As described in the section "Spanish comes to Latin America" in Chapter 3, many indigenous Latin American words have entered Spanish vocabulary as well. The difference is that most of these words have been adopted by Spanish speakers worldwide, but the pronunciation and grammar changes have remained local.

After centuries of second-class citizenship, Latin America's indigenous peoples and their languages have gained increased recognition and status in recent decades. In 1989 almost all Latin American countries ratified the International Labor Organization's "Convention 169," which recognized the importance of indigenous languages worldwide (Slide 4.36). This was followed in 2007 by the United Nation's Declaration on the Rights of Indigenous Peoples (Slide 4.37). As a local reflection of this global movement, more than half the countries in Latin America now recognize indigenous languages in their constitutions, and more than half of these grant the languages co-official status with Spanish, either nationwide or in their respective regions (Slides 4.38–4.40). The 2005 election of Evo Morales (an Aymara from Bolivia) as the first indigenous president of a Latin American country was another manifestation of this trend.

*Teacher talk*

"Latinoamérica es una región de gran diversidad lingüística. Millones de latinoamericanos hablan cientos de idiomas indígenas que pertenecen a docenas de familias lingüísticas distintas. Estos idiomas se han conservado

mayormente en las zonas cuya geografía les desagradaba a los conquistadores, como los territorios que son hoy Bolivia y Paraguay, que no tienen
acceso al mar, las montañas de Perú, y las junglas de Guatemala y Yucatán.
En estas zonas los idiomas indígenas aun han influido la pronunciación y
la gramática de las variedades locales del español. En décadas recientes los
países latinoamericanos han llegado a reconocer y apoyar más sus idiomas
indígenas. Incluso un aymara de Bolivia, Evo Morales, sirvió como presi-
dente de su país durante trece años."

*In-class activities*

- **Estimate or interpret basic statistics about indigenous languages.** In
  this activity students estimate basic statistics about indigenous Latin
  American languages: how many languages there are, how many
  first-language speakers they have, and how many language families they
  belong to. To manage this activity, the teacher clicks on Slide 4.29 to
  hide the numbers, and clicks again to reveal them. (The same animation
  hides and reveals the number of languages spoken before Columbus.)
  Alternatively, with two further clicks on the slide the teacher can present the numbers and ask students to deduce what they refer to.
- **Compare indigenous languages in Latin America and the United States.**
  Many more people speak indigenous languages in Latin America than in
  the United States. As shown in Slide 4.41 (based on Eberhard, Simons, and
  Fennig 2020), of the twenty most-spoken indigenous languages in the two
  areas, the top-ranked language in the United States (Navajo) has fewer
  speakers than the bottom-ranked language in Latin America (Mazatec).
  In this activity, groups of students brainstorm possible reasons for this
  difference, and the class as a whole then evaluates these possibilities.
- **Listen to indigenous languages.** Students listen to videos of people
  speaking different indigenous languages (Slide 4.33). The purpose of the
  activity is simply to expose students to the variety of these languages.
  Teachers can ask students to take notes on frequent sounds, words, or
  word endings in each language as well as sounds that do not occur in
  Spanish or English, and words they recognize from Spanish. As an alternative, students can find and present their own videos (see "Find a
  video of an indigenous language," below).
- **Discuss the challenges of immigration for indigenous language speakers.**
  Students begin by reading a recent article about the special challenges
  faced by Latin American immigrants to New York City who speak
  neither Spanish nor English (*El Diario* 2015). (Teachers may be able to
  find a more recent article, or one about immigrants in their own area.)
  Based on this article, what are the main challenges these immigrants
  face? What resources do they access to address these challenges? Whose
  responsibility is it to help them?

- **Discuss the constitutional status of indigenous languages.** In this activity students read the summary information about Latin American constitutions in Slide 4.38 and the relevant sections from these constitutions in Slides 4.39 and 4.40, then discuss the practical implications of these statutes. For example, for citizens of Ecuador who speak an indigenous language, which "official uses" are likely to affect their lives? Also, what steps should the Ecuadorean government take to "stimulate the conservation and use" of these languages? Many of these constitutions refer to their indigenous languages as *patrimonio cultural*. Are these only words, or do they have a practical side?

  Students can also compare these constitutions to the international standards displayed in Slides 4.36 and 4.37. Do the individual constitutions implement these standards?

  As a preliminary step leading to this activity, students can research the relevant constitutional statutes themselves, as described below in the take-home project "Research language status in Latin American constitutions," instead of the teacher simply presenting the slides.

- **Speak indigenous-influenced Spanish.** Slides 4.34 and 4.35 illustrate how indigenous languages have affected Spanish pronunciation and syntax in parts of Latin America that have a history of bilingualism. To experience first-hand Mayan-influenced pronunciation (Slide 4.34), each pair of students can write a short paragraph (or dialogue) using several words that begin with *f-* and/or end with *-n*. The lists in Slide 4.42 may be helpful. Students should practice saying the paragraph out loud while changing these sounds to *p-* and *-m*, then present it to the class. To experience the Quechuan-influenced changes of *e* and *o* to *i* and *u* (same slide), students can practice and present any Spanish text or dialogue while making these pronunciation changes.

  To experience the Guaraní-influenced syntactic changes in Slide 4.35, each student can write out a list of standard sentences using (i) *haber* or *acabar de* perfects (e.g. *Hemos visto la película* or *Acabo de aprender los verbos*) and (ii) negatives that include a word other than *no* (e.g. <u>Nada</u> *me gusta, No he visto a <u>nadie</u>*) – perhaps three of each type. Students then circulate around the room, challenging their classmates to transform their sentences with Guaraní-style wording.

- **Observe the installation of Evo Morales.** The 2005 election of Evo Morales, Bolivia's first Aymara president, was a significant landmark in the modern history of indigenous peoples in Latin America. After that victory and each subsequent election, Morales followed his formal inauguration with an indigenous ceremony in the Tiwanaku ruins near Lake Titicaca. In this activity, students watch a news report about the ceremony following Morales's 2014 reelection (teleSUR 2015). Afterward, they should discuss with their classmates what they saw: clothing, participants, events, and so on. Finally, students might summarize their observations in a short paragraph; this would be a good opportunity to practice the distinction between the preterite and imperfect past tenses.

*Take-home projects*

- **WebQuest about indigenous languages.** Working alone or in pairs or groups, students complete the WebQuest embedded in Slide 4.43, which is formatted as a quiz. For teachers' reference, correct answers are supplied or marked in red, which should be removed before distributing the document. Teachers may also choose to edit and/or reformat the WebQuest.

  After students complete the WebQuest, the class can review it as a springboard for discussion. For example, the true/false question about Latin American immigrants who do not speak Spanish can lead to a discussion about where these immigrants come from, what language(s) they speak, and what difficulties they are likely to face in the United States. The WebQuest questions can also suggest possible topics for student research or presentations.

- **Profile an indigenous language.** Each student, or group of students, profiles an indigenous language of Latin America. The languages in Slide 4.31 are a useful starting point; however, for greater variety, some of the Mayan languages should be replaced with smaller languages such as Guna (or Kuna), spoken in the San Blas Islands; Garifuna, Purépecha, Miskito, and Tarahumara. The teacher can assign languages or students can choose their own. The completed profile should present the information in Slide 4.44 in the form of a poster, slide presentation, or oral report that students can share with the class.

- **Find a video of an indigenous language.** This project is similar to the preceding one except that the centerpiece of each presentation is a video that the student (or students) finds of someone speaking the assigned language. Besides sharing the video, the student should include some basic information about the language, such as where it is spoken and its number of speakers. Ideally the student will be able to provide some information about the speaker in the video and what they are talking about.

- **Map the most-spoken indigenous languages.** In this activity, students learn where speakers of Latin American indigenous languages primarily live today. The teacher distributes the materials in Slide 4.45: a list of the twenty most-spoken indigenous languages in Latin America and a map (a full-page printout of the map is recommended). As an optional first step, students can estimate in class how many of these languages are probably spoken in each country. At home, students look up the languages and locate them on the map. Afterward, the class compares their maps with the one in Slide 4.31 and discusses the results. The concentration of the languages in specific areas, and their corresponding absence in others, will probably come as a surprise.

- **Research language status in Latin American constitutions.** As a preliminary to the activity "Discuss the constitutional status of indigenous languages," each student looks up the constitution of an assigned Latin American country and any section(s) in the document related to indigenous languages. (Likely search terms within the document are *idioma*, *lengua*, and *bilingüe*.) Students add their findings to a table shared on the Internet (as in Slide 4.46); the teacher should verify this work by comparing it to Slides 4.38–4.40 before the in-class discussion.

### Code-switching

*Just the facts*

When bilingual speakers talk with each other, they may switch back and forth between their shared languages, a practice called code-switching. Research on Spanish code-switching has primarily focused on code-switching with English in the United States. Other languages often code-switched with Spanish include minority languages like Catalan in Spain, indigenous languages like Quechua in Latin America, and Arabic and Berber in Ceuta and Melilla. Some of these pairings are so common that they have their own names, such as *Spanglish* for code-switched Spanish and English in the United States (the term also has other meanings), and *Jopara* for code-switched Spanish and Guarani in Paraguay.

As shown in the Spanish/English examples in Slide 4.47 (based on Moyer 1992; Pfaff 1979; Poplack 1980), switches can involve linguistic units of varying sizes, from full sentences or clauses to individual words. Most switches involve nouns; this is consistent with borrowing between languages, which likewise favors nouns (see Chapter 3). Speakers may make a single switch within a sentence or switch back and forth, a pattern called "congruent lexicalization," as in the last example in the slide.

Spanish/Guarani code-switching is particularly interesting because it often involves Guarani function words and word endings, units of speech that are rarely switched in other language pairings (Slide 4.48). Estigarribia (2017) suggests that speakers add these to their everyday Spanish because they express meanings that are harder to convey in Spanish, just as a speaker of standard American English might resort to a southern *y'all* to compactly express the second person plural. For example, speakers can use the Guarani function word *pa* to create all types of questions: yes/no, "wh," and indirect.

Code-switching requires considerable linguistic skill. While code-switched Spanish/English, for example, might sound to the uninitiated like "bad Spanish" or "bad English," only speakers with a high degree of proficiency in both languages are able to carry it off in a natural fashion. For instance, code-switchers only combine Spanish nouns with English adjectives (or the reverse) when their word order is the same in both languages (Slide 4.49). They also avoid switching certain word types in isolation, such as personal pronouns and question words. Recognizing these permissible and impermissible contexts on the fly requires expertise in both languages (Lipski 2008, 231).

This proficiency is not enough: code-switching also requires that speakers belong to the same social group. For example, it would be bizarre, or even offensive, for an outsider (even if fluent in Spanish) to attempt to code-switch when talking with someone from East Harlem's Puerto Rican community, or with a Chicano from Los Angeles. This would imply a social kinship that does not exist.

### Teacher talk

"Cuando los hablantes bilingües hablan entre sí, pueden pasar con fluidez entre sus dos idiomas. Este fenómeno, que se llama 'cambio de código', se ha observado entre el español y muchos otros idiomas: el inglés en los EE. UU., los idiomas minoritarios en España (como el catalán) y los idiomas indígenas de Latinoamérica (como el quechua). Se pueden cambiar cláusulas enteras, frases, o palabras individuales, a veces múltiples veces dentro de una oración. Para participar en una tal conversación, hace falta hablar bien los dos idiomas y también ser miembro de la misma comunidad lingüística que la persona con quien estás hablando."

### In-class activities

* **Code-switch between Spanish and English.** This activity gives students the chance to try code-switching themselves. Students may simply read out loud the paragraph in Slide 4.50, or another text provided by the teacher (or a student volunteer), while code-switching into English for the underlined portions. For a more challenging task, pairs of students can prepare and practice a short conversation during which they code-switch. A third option is spontaneous: the teacher (or another student) states a conversational situation or theme that a pair of students has to immediately enact while code-switching. Any of these activities can be organized as a competition to see which students can code-switch while sounding most natural, and also respecting the restrictions shown in Slide 4.49.
* **Ask questions using Paraguayan code-switching.** Each student writes six questions using standard Spanish: two yes/no questions, two questions with an interrogative such as *cuándo* or *por qué*, and two indirect

questions. Students then circulate around the room, challenging their classmates to code-switch one of their questions by adding the Guaraní particle *pa* (or *pio*), as in Slide 4.48. For example, *¿Cómo te llamas?* would be code-switched as *¿Cómo pa te llamas?* The first student should then answer the question.

## Language features

### Variation in Spanish pronunciation

*Just the facts*

The examples of variation in Spanish pronunciation in this section flesh out the observation, at the beginning of this chapter, that variation can be a sign of ongoing change in Spanish. We will see several cases of "change from below" (the spread of a non-prestigious variant), such as the deletion of *d* between vowels, and one case of "change from above," the resurgence of the *s/th* distinction in Andalusia.

Some of these ongoing developments continue long-standing currents of phonological change in Spanish (Slide 3.50) and also reflect universal tendencies. For example, the weakening or loss of final -*s* in many Spanish dialects continues the language's history of losing final consonants, as when Latin *iam* became Spanish *ya*, *aliquod* became *algo*, and *dic* became *di*. It also reflects a universal tendency for sounds to be weakened or lost at the ends of words, as in French, where the silent final consonants in *Voulez-vous manger?* memorialize earlier, fuller pronunciations of these words. As another example, the loss of *d* between vowels in words like *cantado* completes a centuries-long process of "lenition," or phonetic weakening, in which Latin *t* between vowels (as in *cantatum*) became *d* (as in *cantado*), then softened to /ð/ (as in English *the*). Again, the same process is seen in other languages, such as the pronunciation of English *writer* with a *d*.

A second observation about the variation examples discussed below is that they all involve consonants, not vowels. This is not a coincidence; the simplicity of the Spanish five-vowel system makes it remarkably stable. When vowels do fluctuate it is either because of outside influence, as in Andean Spanish (Slide 4.34), or as a side-effect of consonant changes, as discussed below in the section on final *s* deletion.

The curious reader will find many other examples of variation in pronunciation discussed in the linguistics literature; either FMOHC (2018), Penny (2000), or Stewart (1999) would be a good starting point.

*Teacher talk*

"Más abajo vamos a considerar unas variaciones en la pronunciación española. Todas tienen que ver con las consonantes, no las vocales. Esto es porque el español solo tiene cinco vocales, un sistema que es muy sencillo y por eso muy estable. Muchas de estas variaciones se encuentran también en otros idiomas."

*In-class activity*

- **Analyze Andalusian wall plaques.** The author photographed the two plaques depicted in Slide 4.51 on walls in the Andalusian city of Cadiz. Each illustrates an important consonant variation discussed below that is typical in Andalusia and is also present in other Spanish-speaking areas. The left-hand plaque includes three examples of final *s* deletion: *escuche*, shortened from *escuches*, *lo* (from *los*), and *madre* (from *madres*). The right-hand plaque contains two examples of *d* deletion between vowels: the words *cantaor* and *bailaor*, which are flamenco terms derived from standard Spanish *cantador* and *bailador*.

  Students can analyze the text in these images as a warm-up activity for the general topic of variation in Spanish pronunciation, or return to them after learning about these specific processes. In the former case, the teacher can ask students to look for what appear to be errors in the plaques' Spanish. In the latter case, the teacher can ask students to find two or three instances of each process.

### *Weakening or deletion of final s*

*Just the facts*

The weakening or deletion ("dropping") of final *s* is one of the best-known characteristics of Spanish pronunciation in Andalusia and parts of Latin America, especially the Caribbean. Speakers may *comerse la ese* in two ways: by weakening it to an *h* ("aspiration") or by dropping it altogether. All syllable-final *s*'s are vulnerable, both within words and at the end of a word. Thus, *estas* might be pronounced as $e^h ta$, with the mid-word *s* aspirated and the word's final *s* deleted. This outcome is more common than the other way around (FMOHC 2018, 506).

The fate of final *s* varies for all the reasons listed at the beginning of this chapter: according to the dialect, social class, age, and gender of a speaker, and the formality of a conversation. Dialectal differences are the most striking. As shown in Slide 4.52, in Spain *s* is retained more often than not in the area around Madrid, but is almost always weakened or lost in the south and southwest (Andalusia and Extremadura) and also the Canary Islands, which group dialectally with Andalusia (Blanco 2004, 174; FMOHC 2018, 506). In Latin America, overall rates of *s* weakening and deletion are highest in the Caribbean, as shown in the slide, and are lowest in Mexico, Guatemala, Costa Rica, and the Andes (Hualde 2005, 23).

Looking beyond dialectal differences, researchers in several countries have found that final *s* is more frequently retained by educated (or upper-class) and older speakers, particularly women, and especially in formal circumstances, as opposed to casual conversation (FMOHC 2018, 510; Penny 2000, 133, 149–50; Silva-Corvalán 2001, 97–98). Slide 4.53 illustrates these factors.

In Murcia and parts of Andalusia, speakers use a more open variant of the vowels *e, a,* and *o* when deleting a final *s*; for example, changing the final *e* of *come(s)* to a more open /ɛ/, as in English *bet* (FMOHC 2018, 510).

Besides the activities below, see also "Analyzing Andalusian wall plaques," above.

*Teacher talk*

"En muchas partes del mundo hispano es muy común comerse (eliminar) la *ese* al final de una sílaba o palabra: por ejemplo pronunciar *estas* como *e^hta*. Tal pronunciación originó en el sur de España, de donde se ha extendido a las Islas Canarias y partes de Latinoamérica, sobre todo el Caribe. Se come más la *ese* en el habla de la gente maleducada o de la clase obrera, en el habla de los jóvenes y los hombres y en conversaciones informales. "

*In-class activities*

- **Listen to final *s*.** Slide 4.54 contains a link to a video of a presentation by the Puerto Rican author Magali García Ramis (Prensa RUM 2013). Students watch a short portion of the video, taking notes on how García pronounces the words listed on the slide. Is each *s* pronounced fully, as an *h*, or deleted? Afterward, students can compare notes and observations.

- **Discuss factors in variation.** Using Slide 4.53 as a starting point, groups of students discuss why certain speaker characteristics or speech situations affect pronunciation. Given that the retention of *s* is considered more prestigious, why does it follow that women and older people would be less likely to drop their *s*'s, and that *s* is retained more in formal contexts? What aspects of English pronunciation exhibit a similar pattern?

  Of course, these sociological factors interact with dialect. For example, students who complete the activity "Listen to final *s*" just above will have observed that García Ramis drops many *s*'s even though, as an older, educated woman speaking formally, she meets all the criteria shown in Slide 4.53. However, relative to Puerto Rican speakers in general her pronunciation of *s* is moderate.

*Take-home project*

• **Ask a native speaker about *s* deletion.** This activity requires students to work with a native speaker partner as described in the Introduction. Each student should ask their partner about *s* deletion in his or her own dialect of Spanish and/or other dialects. Slide 4.55 includes sample questions, or the class can develop its own list. Students can summarize their findings in a written, oral, or graphic report.

## Yeísmo, seseo, and ceceo

*Just the facts*

These three variations in the pronunciation of Spanish consonants are so well-known that they have their own names (Slide 4.56). *Yeísmo* refers to a merger between the *y* of *haya* and the *ll* of *halla*, while *seseo* and *ceceo* refer to two possible pronunciations of the *s* of *casa* and the *z* of *caza*. In *seseo*, both sounds are pronounced *s*; in *ceceo*, both are pronounced with a sound close to *th*. As noted in Chapter 3, dialects with *seseo* did not lose the *th*; rather, they never acquired it (see "The sound changes that shaped Spanish words" and Slide 3.52).

As with *s*-deletion, one's dialect strongly affects these pronunciation variations. *Yeísmo* has spread through most of the Spanish-speaking world: *y* and *ll* are still distinguished only in northern Spain and the Andes, the latter probably due to influence from indigenous languages that happen to have the *ll* sound (Penny 2000, 147–48). In most *yeísta* regions the *y* and *ll* sounds have coalesced as *y*, but other possible pronunciations include /ʒ/ as in *pleasure* and *sh*, most famously in the Rio Plate area (coastal Argentina and Uruguay). *Seseo* is common in Andalusia, where it originated, and is the norm throughout Latin America. *Ceceo* is a later development found mostly in coastal areas of Andalusia (Penny 2000, 118–20).

*Yeísmo* and *seseo/ceceo* in Spain are excellent examples of "change from below" and "change from above," respectively, as described above. Traditionally, the distinctions between *y* and *ll*, and between *s* and *th*, have both been perceived as prestigious. The continued northward march of *yeísmo* is thus a change from below – that is, going against a prestige form. (In fact, the victory of *yeísmo* is so complete that speakers in *yeísta* areas no longer perceive the *y/ll* contrast as prestigious (Stewart 1999, 49).) In contrast, the *s/th* distinction has been resurging in Andalusia in recent decades at the expense of both *seseo* and *ceceo*: a change from above. Both the advance in *yeísmo* and the retreat of *seseo* and *ceceo* have been spearheaded by young urban speakers; for *seseo* and *ceceo*, education is another factor, with more educated speakers favoring the Castilian contrast (FMOHC 2018, 502–5).

For *yeísmo*, the specific pronunciation of the merged consonant also has social meaning. As mentioned above, in the Rio Plate area the usual outcome of the merger is /ʒ/ or *sh* rather than *y*. Today the *sh* variant has taken over Buenos Aires, and younger people, especially women, are driving it into the surrounding area (Michnowicz and Planchón 2020, 177).

For a global perspective on the *th* sound, see Chapter 1.

### Teacher talk

"El español tradicional de Castilia hace una distinción entre la *y* de *cayó* y la *ll* de *calló*, y entre la *s* de *casa* y la *th* de *caza*. Muchos dialectos del español, sobre todo en el sur de España y en Latinoamérica, no tienen estas diferencias. En unos dialectos la pronunciación de las consonantes relevantes es estable pero en otros su pronunciación depende de las características personales de un hablante, como su edad, su sexo y su educación, y también depende de la formalidad de una conversación."

### In-class activities

- **Listen to *yeísmo* (or the *y/ll* contrast).** This activity requires some set-up time on the part of the instructor (or students: see the corresponding take-home project). The teacher starts by visiting the website forvo. com and listening to individual recordings of words such as *caballo* (Slide 4.57). The goal is to select a set of recordings whose pronunciation of *ll* varies, ideally including multiple instances of *ll*, *y*, /ʒ/ as in *pleasure*, and *sh*. Each Forvo recording indicates the speaker's nationality; for this activity, speakers from Argentina are particularly interesting.

  In class, the teacher should play each recording two or three times and ask students to note the pronunciation of each written *ll*, perhaps filling out a sheet such as the one in Slide 4.58. Afterward, besides comparing their judgments with each other and with the teacher, students can make general observations about the pronunciations they heard from different countries. They can also discuss any difficulty they faced in accomplishing this listening task.
- **Practice *seseo*, *ceceo*, and the *s/th* contrast with tongue twisters.** This activity brings home the reality of these three variant pronunciation styles. Students practice and recite one, some, or all of the four tongue twisters shown in Slide 4.59. This activity may be structured in various ways; for example, the class could be divided into "Equipo *seseo*," "Equipo *ceceo*," and "Equipo *distinción*," who compete for the best recitations. Or individual students may be challenged to spontaneously recite a given tongue twister with a given pronunciation style.

### Take-home project

- **Find examples of *yeísmo* (or the *y/ll* contrast).** This activity replaces the teacher's set-up process for the corresponding in-class activity described above. Each student (or pair of students) is assigned a word from Slide 4.57

to research on forvo.com. Their goal is to select a set of recordings that run the gamut for their assigned word, ideally including *ll*, *y*, /ʒ/ as in *pleasure*, and *sh*. For this reason, it is important for students to indicate the consonant they heard for each recording they selected. The teacher reviews these examples, then runs the in-class portion of the activity as described above.

Hopefully, as they select their recordings, the students will serendipitously observe other interesting aspects of regional variation in pronunciation. These can also be reviewed in class.

### Deleting d between vowels

*Just the facts*

Deletion of *d* between two vowels, especially in past participles like *hablado* and *comido*, is another well-known example of Spanish consonant variation that depends on both dialectal and social factors. It is most common in Andalusia and least common in Latin America (Slide 4.60). Within Spain, the northward spread of *d* deletion has all the hallmarks of a "change from below." That is, the pronunciation is spreading even though maintaining the *d* is traditionally seen as more "correct" as in, for example, Telemadrid's (1993) style guide (Slide 4.61), and deletion is more common among Spaniards who are in general less educated, male, younger, and/or speaking casually (Stewart 1999, 46–47).

*Teacher talk*

"En el habla popular, sobre todo en Andalusia, es común eliminar la *d* entre vocales en palabras como *hablado*. Esta pronunciación tradicionalmente se ha considerado incorrecta por la cual ocurre más en el habla de jóvenes, de varones, de gente menos educada y en situaciones informales."

*In-class activities*

* **Listen to -*ao* and -*io*.** Hearing some examples of -*ado* and -*ido* pronounced without a *d* is a good way to introduce this topic. However, because *d* deletion is most common in casual speech, it can be hard to find recorded examples that Spanish students can hear clearly. Slide 4.62 links to a pair of YouTube videos that can fill this gap. The first is short and humorous; the second is straightforward, and also includes clearly enunciated examples of other Andalusian phonetic processes. The teacher can present these videos or have a student take on this role.
* **Debate the linguistic relevance of mass media.** As a warm-up to this activity, students should compare three slides that reveal a contradiction that is common for "changes from below." On the one hand, Spaniards (and, to some extent, other Spanish speakers) often delete *d* between vowels (Slide 4.60). This is especially the case in Andalusia, where *d*

deletion has even been enshrined in the vocabulary of Andalusia's own form of music and dance, the flamenco (Slide 4.51). On the other hand, the Spanish mass media have, at least in the past, frowned on *d* deletion (Slide 4.61). This raises the question: how important are mass media in promulgating linguistic standards, especially in the Internet era?

Slide 4.63 lists some discussion questions along these lines that groups of students or the whole class can consider.

### The Puerto Rican r

*Just the facts*

Some Puerto Ricans pronounce the *r* in the back of the mouth, as in French, instead of the front as is standard. This is an example of a non-prestige variant that has attained local prestige by becoming an emblem of group identity. Accordingly, while speakers generally suppress non-prestige variants in careful speech (for example, taking care to pronounce *d*'s between vowels), speakers who use the Puerto Rican *r* tend to favor it in all speech settings (Lipski 2008, 124). The quotation in Slide 4.64, from *La R de mi padre* (García Ramis 2011), summarizes the push-and-pull of traditional and local prestige.

*Teacher talk*

"Unos puertorriqueños pronuncian la *erre* como los franceses, con la parte posterior de la lengua. Aunque tradicionalmente esta pronunciación se considera incorrecta, en Puerto Rico muchas personal la ven como un símbolo lingüístico de su identidad."

*In-class activity*

• **Listen to the Puerto Rican r.** A video of García Ramis speaking at the Recinto Universitario de Mayagüez includes explicit examples of this *r* variant at 0:40 and 4:50 (Slide 4.65, Prensa RUM 2013). The class can try to imitate it.
• **Compare perspectives on the Puerto Rican r.** The passage from García Ramis (2011) in Slide 4.64 captures her childhood memories of how different people felt about this variant pronunciation: young people (including García Ramis), who embraced it, older family members and schoolteachers, who opposed it, and her father, who brought it into the family. Students should first read the selection with help from their teacher (and optionally, the vocabulary glosses in Slide 4.66). In a class discussion, students can then identify and contrast these three perspectives.

The class might also discuss García Ramis's analogy between the *r* variant and Puerto Rico itself. How are they similar? What variant pronunciations of English sounds are likewise strong markers of regional identity and pride?

## Vocabulary

### Just the facts

Spanish dialects often use different words to refer to the same thing, or use the same word to refer to different things (Slides 4.67 and 4.68).

How do dialects come to use different words? In some cases, dialectal words simply descend from alternative Latin roots. For example, *melocotón* comes from Latin *malum cotonium* (originally, a cross between a peach and a quince) but *durazno* evolved from *duracinus* (originally, stone fruit more generally). *Campera* is a natural extension of *campo* since one wears a jacket when outside. Some variants come from different languages: *aguacate* is from Nahuatl, while *palta* is Quichua. Other sources of dialectal vocabulary include onomatopoeia and proper nouns. Thus *chucho*, in its original meaning of 'mutt,' comes from the sound one makes when calling a dog, and *birome*, a word for 'pen' used in parts of South America, was an early Argentinian brand name.

How do dialects come to ascribe different meanings to the same words? Essentially, such changes in meaning follow the same semantic pathways as changes in meaning more generally (see Chapter 3). For example, words often take on a negative connotation, as when *chucho* came to mean 'stingy' in some dialects (Slide 4.68). *Calabaza* and *capulla* can both mean 'idiot, dolt,' while *fresa* can be 'preppy' (in a negative sense), and *coger* is obscene in much of Latin America. Words can also take on a positive connotation, as when *tío* came to mean 'pal' in Spain. Contact with other languages can also foster change; the takeover of *carro* from *coche* in Latin America shows English influence, for instance.

### Teacher talk

"Hay bastantes diferencias entre el vocabulario en los diferentes dialectos del español. Los dialectos pueden usar diferentes palabras; por ejemplo, se dice *computadora* en Latinoamérica pero *ordenador* en España. Según tu país se hace el guacamole con *aguacate* o *palta* y se celebra el cumpleaños con un *pastel*, una *torta* o un *queque*. También el sentido de una palabra puede variar entre países. Un *guagua* es un bebé en partes de Latinoamérica y un autobús en otros; una *tortilla* se hace con huevos y papas en España pero con maíz o trigo en Latinoamérica."

### In-class activities

*   **Maintain a word board or map.** During a semester or year, whenever students learn dialectal vocabulary, they can add the words to a corkboard or whiteboard display, either in list form or on a map. For example, when they learn *piscina*, they can pin that word (perhaps including a

picture) to a map of Spain and likewise *pileta* to Argentina and *alberca* to Mexico. The class could also maintain a list or map online.

• **Use dialectal vocabulary.** Students create and present dialogues featuring dialectal vocabulary, using words from Slides 4.67 and 4.68, or from one of the take-home activities below. The two participants might use words from the same dialect; for example, they could both play the role of Argentinians, using several words specific to that country or to Latin America more generally. Or each participant could choose to represent a different dialect…which could lead to humorous misunderstandings.

*Take-home projects*

• **Trace dialectal variants to their countries.** Students use wordreference. com or another resource to identify the countries where speakers use the different words listed in Slide 4.67; for example, where speakers say *acera, andén, banqueta,* or *vereda* for 'sidewalk.' They can record their work by annotating a copy of the slide.

• **Find dialectal variants for a list of meanings.** Students use wordreference. com or another resource to find the words that speakers use in different dialects to express the same meanings. Students might all look up different words for the eight meanings in Slide 4.67 (avocado, car, peach, etc.) The class can then compare the words they find with those shown on the graphic. Alternatively, the teacher can assign each student some of the meanings from the longer list in Slide 4.69. If students record their results in a shared spreadsheet, including the countries where the different words are used, the class can then use this spreadsheet for the in-class activity "Use dialectal vocabulary."

• **Find dialectal vocabulary via the Internet.** In this activity, instead of working from a list of words or word meanings, students explore the Internet on their own to find dialectal vocabulary to share with the class. The teacher can assign each student a different country, in which case the students can use search terms like "vocabulario dialectal de Argentina." Alternatively, students can find more general information using search terms like "vocabulario diferente" or "palabras diferentes en español." In class, students can combine the results of their research to create a master list that they can use for the activity "Use dialectal vocabulary."

• **Ask a native speaker about vocabulary from their country.** This activity requires students to work with a native speaker partner as described in the Introduction. Each student should ask their partner about words spoken in their country that are different from those in other countries. A possible way to phrase this question is simply *¿Cuáles son unas palabras únicas de tu país?* To broaden the activity, students could ask about other countries as well: *¿y en otros países?* Students can summarize their findings in a written, oral, or graphic report. Alternatively, as with the previous activity, students can pool their results to create a master list that can be used for the activity "Use dialectal vocabulary."

## Leísmo

*Just the facts*

Spanish third person object pronouns are genuinely complex. First, they are the only object pronouns that distinguish direct and indirect objects, whereas *me*, *te*, *nos*, and *os* all do double duty. Second, *lo/la* and *los/las* are the only object pronouns that mark gender. Third, while direct objects are usually things, and indirect objects are usually people, this is not a reliable distinction, especially for direct objects (e.g. *Lo admiro* 'I admire him').

Therefore, it is not surprising that the use of third-person object pronouns varies according to dialect and also social factors. Simplifying the dialectal situation somewhat, Latin Americans generally follow the system described above, whereas Spaniards (especially in the north) practice *leísmo*, meaning that they use *le* and *les* instead of *lo* and *los* as masculine direct object pronouns **when referring to humans** (Slide 4.70). This *leísmo* is different from the so-called *leísmo de cortesía* that substitutes *le/s* for *lo/s* and *la/s* when referring to *usted(es)*, as in *Señor, le agradezco sinceramente*.

Other variations on the two basic systems in the slide, again found mostly in Spain, include *laísmo* and *loísmo* (using *la(s)* and *lo(s)* as indirect as well as direct object pronouns) and a more vigorous form of *leísmo* in which *le* and *les* serve as masculine direct pronouns whether or not they refer to humans.

In terms of social factors, the long-standard prestige of Castilian Spanish has caused Latin American Spanish to drift slightly toward *leísmo* in the written language and in "cultured speech," a trend noticed as early as the mid-twentieth century (Kany 1945, 102). Within Spain, *laísmo*, *loísmo*, and extended *leísmo* are disfavored and therefore losing ground to the version of *leísmo* shown in Slide 4.70 – a change "from above."

*Teacher talk*

"En España es bastante común usar *le* y *les* en vez de *lo* y *los* cuando se refieren a seres humanos: por ejemplo, *Le admiro* en vez de *Lo admiro* cuando hablas de tu papá. Este uso es más común en el norte de España aunque se encuentra más y más en el sur, y también en el español latinoamericano escrito."

*In-class activities*

- **Answer questions with (or without)** *leísmo.* In this activity, students answer questions using direct object pronouns according to *leísmo*; that is, using *le* and *les* as masculine direct object pronouns when referring to humans. Students may simply answer the questions in Slide 4.71. (Note: some have feminine direct objects.) For a more challenging activity, students can first write their own questions, then circulate around the room eliciting answers from other students. For even greater interest, half the class could be designated *leísta* and half non-*leísta*, and answer questions accordingly, perhaps switching their designation halfway through the activity. As with *tú* and *usted* (Chapter 1), students can put on a tie to show that they are *leísta*.
- **Examine changing standards for object pronouns.** *Leísmo* is not a modern deviation from the standard object pronoun system shown at the top of Slide 4.70; rather, some form of *leísmo* has been present in Spain for centuries. In fact, the evolving attitude of the Real Academia Española toward *leísmo* provides an excellent example of how language standards can change over time. An advanced Spanish class could read and discuss the relevant excerpts in Slides 4.72–4.74, from RAE 1796 and 1854.

  As shown in Slide 4.72, through the end of the eighteenth century, the Academia's *Gramática* advocated extreme *leísmo*, entirely ruling out *lo* as a masculine singular direct object pronoun. The academicians even criticized Cervantes and other authors for using *lo*, attributing this practice to faulty copyediting, authorial carelessness, or excessive attention to aesthetic considerations. *Lo* was only recognized as a legitimate alternative to *le* in the mid-nineteenth century, at which time the academicians praised, but did not endorse, the modern Castilian standard (Slide 4.73). Throughout this time period, the Academia lamented the wide variation in usage of these pronouns (Slide 4.74).

## Subject pronouns

*Just the facts*

Spanish speakers around the world differ in the subject pronouns they use to express 'you.' Most Latin Americans use the two singular pronouns *tú* and *usted* and the plural pronoun *ustedes*. Spaniards add the informal plural *vosotros*, while most Central Americans, as well as Argentinians and their neighbors, and Mexicans in Chiapas, replace (or supplement) *tú* with the informal singular *vos*. The animations in Slide 4.75 illustrate these three variations. *Vos* verb endings (Slide 4.76) descend from Latin's and vary somewhat among dialects. For example, in the future tense, many dialects use the standard *tú* ending *-ás* instead of *-és*.

The apparently scattershot geographic patterning of *voseo* has a simple historical explanation (Slide 4.77, based on Penny 2000, 152–53). As described in the in-class activity "Trace the development of the Spanish 'you' pronouns" (Slide 2.20), during the colonial period Spaniards commonly used both *tú* and *vos* (originally a plural 'you') as informal singulars. As *tú* came to dominate in Spain, it did so also in parts of Latin America that were in frequent contact with Spain: the Caribbean, Panama (as the bridge between the Caribbean and the Pacific), and the areas around the two colonial capitals of Mexico City and Lima. *Vos* continued to dominate only in parts of Latin America that were relatively remote.

For speakers of *voseo* dialects, this aspect of Spanish grammar can serve as a symbol of local identity and pride, like the Buenos Aires version of *yeísmo* and the Puerto Rican *r*, both discussed above. Slide 4.78 presents one Costa Rican writer's defense of *voseo* (Mora Poltronieri 2011).

Spanish dialects also differ in how they use the standard pronouns (Slide 4.79). Spaniards notoriously use *tú* (and *vosotros*) more than *usted* (and *ustedes*), even when addressing older people. Slide 4.80 presents one writer's vivid description of this phenomenon (González Castro 2007). On the other hand, many Colombians use *usted* instead of *tú* when talking with intimate friends and family members (Uber 1985); Slide 4.81 shows some cinematic examples. Both these departures from standard use of *tú* and *usted* can be quite unsettling for an outsider to hear, and even more so to emulate.

See Chapter 2 for a cross-linguistic perspective on these pronouns.

### Teacher talk

"En nuestra clase practicamos los tres pronombres típicos de Latinoamérica que expresan el concepto de 'you': *tú, usted* y *ustedes*. Pero varios países usan otros pronombres. En España se usa *vosotros* como plural informal; en Centroamérica, Argentina y otros países sudamericanos se usa *vos* como alternativa a *tú*. Además, diferentes países usan sus pronombres de maneras diferentes. En España casi nunca se usa *usted*, mientras en Colombia se usa mucho, incluso con parientes, amigos y novios."

### In-class activities

• **Infer nationalities from dialogues.** After viewing and discussing Slides 4.75 (on pronoun inventories), 4.76 (on *voseo*), and 4.79 (on *tú/usted* usage in Spain and Colombia), pairs of students prepare and present brief dialogues that simulate a conversation between two speakers from one of the relevant countries, choosing situations that highlight "their" country's distinctive 'you' pronouns and associated verb forms. Some possibilities might be a Spanish college student using *tú* in a conversation with a professor, a Colombian girl using *usted* when chatting with her boyfriend, or Argentinian teenagers using *voseo* when planning a get-together. After each pair presents their dialogue, their classmates try to identify their country.

- **Discuss readings on *voseo* and *tuteo*.** The readings on Costa Rican *voseo* and Spanish *tuteo* (Slides 4.78 and 4.80) are interesting in and of themselves as pieces of writing. Either can also spark class discussion on the relationship between language and identity. Does any aspect of the English language inspire such passion?
- **Observe intimate Colombian *usted*.** Students read the movie quotes in Slide 4.81 and attempt to identify what is unusual about the language. This would be a natural introduction to the topic of dialectal variation in the use of basic pronouns.

### Take-home project

- **Ask a native speaker about dialectal pronoun differences.** This activity requires students to work with a native speaker partner as described in the Introduction. While the related project "Ask a native speaker about their pronoun usage" in Chapter 2 focused on the partner's own pronoun usage, this one asks for the partner's insights into usage more generally, in the partner's own dialect and others. Suggested questions are in Slide 4.82. Students can summarize their findings in a written, oral, or graphic report.

## Non-standard verb forms

### Just the facts

Preterite *tú* forms with an added *-s*, such as *\*Tú hablastes español*, and *haber* existentials with an added plural *-n*, as in *\*Habían tres muchachas* or *\*Habrán muchas fiestas*, are non-standard but logical outgrowths of the standard Spanish verb system. Because all other *tú* forms end with an *s* (e.g. *hablas, hablabas, hablarás*), it is natural for Spanish speakers to add an *-s* to the preterite. In fact, examples of such forms can be found as far back as the 1500s (Slide 4.83). Likewise, every verb but *haber* appears in the plural when its subject is plural, so it is natural to aim for a plural existential as well. (See Hochberg (2016, 266) for a historical explanation of this oddity.) Forms like *habían* and *habrán* already exist as auxiliaries, making it easy to repurpose them as plural existentials, but the Real Academia Española has even noted cases of a novel plural existential for the present tense: *\*hayn*, as in *\*En el centro también hayn cafés* (RAE 2005).

Preterite *-s* is the only example of variation in this chapter that is not affected by dialect. Instead, its controlling factor is education: throughout the Spanish-speaking world, less-educated Spanish speakers are most likely to use verb forms like *hablastes and *comistes. Education also affects speakers' use of plural existentials, although in certain areas, including Catalonia, Caracas, Santiago de Chile, and Buenos Aires, speakers of all classes regularly use them (Penny 2000, 220; Stewart 1999, 96–97).

### Teacher talk

"Muchos hispanohablantes, sobre todo los con menos educación, usan formas verbales que son lógicas pero no son estándares. Primero, como las formas *tú* del pretérito, por ejemplo *hablaste* y *comiste*, son las únicas formas de *tú* que no terminan con *ese*, mucha gente dice *hablastes* y *comistes*, añadiendo una *ese* final. También, como no parece lógico decir, por ejemplo, *Había tres pruebas en el semestre*, mucha gente dice *Habían tres pruebas*, añadiendo una *ene* plural aunque no es estándar."

### In-class activity

*   **Interpret non-standard verb forms.** The teacher shows the examples of non-standard verb forms in Slide 4.84. Students work in pairs to identify what aspects of these verbs are non-standard, and to deduce why speakers make these "mistakes." They share their ideas with the class.
    A class discussion can also take up the deeper question of whether language uses should be considered "right/correct" versus "wrong/incorrect/mistakes" or instead, merely "standard" versus "non-standard."

### Variation in verb use

### Just the facts

Speakers of different Spanish dialects vary in how they use two pairs of closely related verb tenses: the conjugated and *ir a* futures, and the preterite and present perfect. In general, Latin American speakers use the *ir a* future more than Spaniards, and Spaniards use the present perfect, as well as other perfect tenses, more than Latin Americans (Slide 4.85).

As discussed in Chapter 3 ("The evolution of the Spanish verb system"), the *ir a* future and the present perfect are both relatively new tenses, and history teaches us that such tenses often eventually replace older ones. For example, modern spoken French has phased out its version of the preterite (the *passé simple*) and relies entirely its version of the present perfect (the *passé composé*). The replacement of Latin's original future tense conjugation by the Romance conjugations based on *haber(e)* is another good example of this phenomenon (Slide 3.75). Looked at this way, Latin Americans and Spaniards are leading the vanguard for a possible eventual phase-out of the conjugated future and the preterite, respectively.

See Chapter 1 for the take-home project "Quantify past tense usage," which can be tailored to include a contrasting analysis of Spanish and Latin American newspaper articles.

*Teacher talk*

"Hay diferencias dialectales en la expresión del futuro y del pasado. En Latinoamérica los eventos futuros se expresan con la construcción *ir a* más que en España, mientras en España los eventos pasados se expresan con el presente perfecto más que en Latinoamérica."

*Take-home project*

• **Ask a native speaker about future tense usage.** This activity requires students to work with a native speaker partner as described in the Introduction. Each student should ask their partner about their own usage of the conjugated and *ir a* futures. This can be as simple as asking whether they are more likely to say *Voy a estudiar* or *Estudiaré*, as elaborate as constructing a fill-in-the-blank questionnaire with a variety of subjects, verbs, and time frames (like *mañana* or *algún día*), or something in between. The results will be particularly interesting if students' partners come from a variety of Spanish-speaking countries.

The following references are cited in this chapter's text and/or its accompanying PowerPoint presentation.

## References

Blanco, M. 2004. *Estudio sociolingüístico de Alcalá de Henares.* Alcalá de Henares: Universidad de Alcalá.

Eberhard, D. M., G. F. Simons, and D. D. Fennig, eds. 2020. *Ethnologue: Languages of the world.* 23rd ed. Dallas, TX: SIL International. Online version: http://www.ethnologue.com.

*El Diario.* 2015. Inmigrantes indígenas chocan con barreras del idioma. August 7.

Estigarribia, B. 2017. Guarani morphology in Paraguayan Spanish: Insights from code-mixing typology. *Hispania* 100: 47–64.

European Commission. 2012. *Europeans and their languages.* Special Eurobarometer 386. Brussels: Directorate-General Communication (European Commission). https://ec.europa.eu/commfrontoffice/publicopinion/archives/ebs/ebs_386_en.pdf.

Fernández de Molina Ortés, E., and J. M. Hernández-Campoy (FMOHC). 2018. Geographic varieties of Spanish. In *The Cambridge handbook of Spanish linguistics*, ed. K. L. Geeslin, 496–528. Cambridge: Cambridge University Press.

García Ramis, M. 2011. La R de mi padre. In *La R de mi padre y otras letras familiares*, 7–38. San Juan, Puerto Rico: Ediciones Callejón.

González Castro, A. 2007. Ni usted ni sopas. *El ciervo: Revista de pensamiento y cultura*, 671. http://elciervo.simply-webspace.es/index.php/archivo/3044-2007/numero-671/438-alias_513.

Granda, G. de. 1979. Calcos sintácticos del guaraní en el español del Paraguay. *Nueva Revista de Filología Hispanica* 28: 267–86.

Hochberg, G. 2016. *¿Por qué? 101 questions about Spanish*. London: Bloomsbury.

Hualde, J. I. 2005. *The sounds of Spanish*. Cambridge: Cambridge University Press.

Kany, C. E. 1945. *Spanish-American syntax*. Chicago, IL: University Chicago Press.

Labov, W. 1963. The social motivation of a sound change. *Word* 19: 273–309. Reprinted in *Sociolinguistic patterns*, 1–42. Philadelphia: University of Pennsylvania Press, 1972.

Lipski, J. M. 1994. *Latin American Spanish*. London: Longman.

———. 1996. *El español de América*. Madrid: Cátedra.

———. 2008. *Varieties of Spanish in the United States*. Georgetown: Georgetown University Press.

Mackenzie, I. 1999–2020. *The linguistics of Spanish*. http://www.staff.ncl.ac.uk/i.e.mackenzie/index.html (homepage).

Michnowicz, J., and Planchón, L. 2020. Sheísmo in Montevideo Spanish. In *Variation and evolution: Aspects of language contact and contrast across the Spanish-speaking world*, eds. S. Sessarego, J. J. Colomina-Almiñana, and A. Rodríguez-Riccelli, 163–86. Amsterdam: John Benjamin.

Mora Poltronieri, H. 2011. ¿Eres tico...o sos todavía tico? *La Nación*, September 14.

Moyer, M. G. 1992. *Analysis of code-switching in Gibraltar*. PhD diss., Universitat Autònoma de Barcelona.

Penny, R. 2000. *Variation and change in Spanish*. Cambridge: Cambridge University Press.

———. 2002. *A history of the Spanish language*. 2nd ed. Cambridge: Cambridge University Press.

Pfaff, C. W. 1979. Constraints on language mixing: Intrasentential code-switching and borrowing in Spanish/English. *Language* 55: 291–318.

Pharies, D. A. 2007. *A brief history of the Spanish language*. Chicago, IL: University of Chicago Press.

Poplack, S. 1980. Sometimes I'll start a sentence in Spanish Y TERMINO EN ESPAÑOL: Toward a typology of code-switching. *Linguistics* 18: 581–618.

*Prensa RUM*. 2013. *Presentan libro de la escritora García Ramis en el RUM*. https://www.youtube.com/watch?v=mzI4F5KMvL0&ab_channel=PrensaRUM.

Real Academia Española (RAE). 1796. *Gramática de la lengua castellana*, 4th ed. Madrid: Viuda de Ibarra. https://books.google.com/books?id=iLIGAAAAQAAJ.

———. 1854. *Gramática de la lengua castellana*, 5th ed. Madrid: Imprenta Nacional. https://books.google.com/books?id=Q7mCUYpiesQC.

———. 2005. *Diccionario panhispánico de dudas*. https://www.rae.es/dpd/.

———. n.d. Banco de datos (CORDE). *Corpus diacrónico del español*. http://corpus.rae.es/cordenet.html.

Silva-Corvalán, C. 2001. *Sociolingüística y pragmática del español*. Washington, DC: Georgetown University Press.

Stewart, M. 1999. *The Spanish language today*. London: Routledge.

Telemadrid. 1993. *Libro de estilo de Telemadrid*. Madrid: Ediciones Telemadrid.

*teleSUR*. 2015. Evo Morales es investido como líder de los pueblos indígenas. January 21. https://www.youtube.com/watch?v=TqtzvD-QXE4.

Uber, D. R. 1985. The dual function of *usted*: Forms of address in Bogotá Colombia. *Hispania* 68(2): 388–92.

Whitehead, N. L. 1999. The crises and transformations of invaded societies: The Caribbean (1492–1580). In *The Cambridge history of the native peoples of the Americas Vol. 3: South America, Part 1*, eds. F. Salomon and S. B. Schwartz, 864–903. Cambridge: Cambridge University Press.

# Chapter 5

# How do people learn and use Spanish?

How do people learn Spanish? And how does the human mind organize and process the language, once learned? The field of psycholinguistics addresses these and other questions, and the resulting insights can play several roles in the classroom.

To begin with, the fact that children often experience the same difficulties with Spanish that they do can reassure students that they, too, will eventually be able to master the language. For example, children's verb conjugation mistakes are similar to those of Spanish students. This shows that the verb system is both genuinely challenging and ultimately learnable. Second, students can identify interesting (and even endearing) commonalities between children's acquisition of Spanish and their own acquisition of English, such as the special way that parents speak to babies, and the nature of children's first words. These can spark thought and discussion about the nature of language acquisition in general. Finally, research that demonstrates the psychological reality of key aspects of Spanish, from syllable structure to grammatical gender, will impress students with the importance of these features.

The chapter first takes up the topic of language acquisition. After a preliminary look at *lenguaje de bebé*, the variety of Spanish that caretakers use when speaking to children, it focuses on how children learn Spanish sounds, words, and grammar. Activities in this section give students the opportunity to **analyze** actual examples of children's speech, as well as data extracted from a variety of acquisition studies. Many of the latter focus on children's typical errors in pronunciation (e.g. *\*uper* for *super*), words (e.g. extending *guaguau* 'doggy' to other animals), and grammar (e.g. *\*sabo* for *sé*). Activities related to second language acquisition are largely **introspective**: for example, brainstorming on how one might approach a given topic using different learning modalities (visual, auditory, and so on), or comparing children's acquisition process with their own.

The second part of the chapter covers some diverse types of evidence that linguists have brought to bear on speakers' knowledge and use of their own language: speech errors, laboratory studies, and Spanish "Pig Latin" (*jerigonzas*). Students again have the chance to analyze data, such as actual speech errors, or to **engage** with these topics themselves by speaking a *jerigonza* or reproducing an experiment involving memory and grammatical gender.

Many topics in this chapter are of interest to the average Spanish speaker. Therefore, in several activities students **ask a native speaker** about their own experiences with these topics.

For a full list of the chapter's activities and projects, and their suitability for different levels of instruction, see Appendices A and B.

## Learning Spanish

### Motherese ("baby talk")

*Just the facts*

Like English-speaking parents, Spanish-speaking parents use a special style of language, which linguists call "motherese," when talking to their babies (Slide 5.1). Parents use words not normally heard in speech to adults, change the sounds and/or structure of normal words, and speak with an overall higher pitch, with exaggerated intonational ups and downs. Most of these changes do not necessarily help children learn to talk; rather, they have evolved as canonical adult imitations of young children's own speech. However, the high pitch and varied intonation of baby talk correspond to infants' perceptual abilities and are therefore well suited to catching and holding their attention (Sachs 1979).

*Teacher talk*

"Los padres hispanohablantes hablan a sus bebés de una manera única. En este 'lenguaje de bebé' se usan algunas palabras especiales, se modifican las palabras normales y se emplea una entonación alta y variada, con subidas y bajadas dramáticas. Es parecida a la forma en que hablan los padres de habla inglesa."

*In-class activities*

- **Analyze words from motherese**. In this activity students work in pairs or groups to discern patterns in some words used in *lenguaje de bebé* (Slide 5.2) and to find similarities between these and typical features of motherese in English. Class discussion can focus on why people speak this way to babies, and whether it is likely to help babies learn.
- **Observe motherese videos**. Students watch and take notes on videos of parents speaking Spanish to their babies, looking for the features in Slide 5.1 and observing any interesting additional features. Slide 5.3

links to four such videos along with some notes. Students should find that the parents in all four videos use the characteristic intonation pattern of motherese. They will also hear special vocabulary, diminutives, and a consonant substitution (*¿Qué pasha?* for *¿Qué pasa?*). Afterward, students can compare and discuss what they observed.

### Take-home project

- **Ask a native speaker about motherese.** This activity requires students to work with a native speaker partner as described in the Introduction. Each student should ask their partner how people talk to babies in Spanish. It will be helpful to ask the partner to produce a simulated example of Spanish motherese by pretending they are talking to a baby. Students can summarize their findings in a written, oral, or graphic report.

## Order of acquisition of consonants

### Just the facts

Children typically learn Spanish consonants in the order shown in Slide 5.4, which is based on McLeod and Crowe's survey of consonant acquisition in twenty-seven languages including Spanish and English (2018). For Spanish, McLeod and Crowe combined data from four studies that involved a total of 420 children growing up in a variety of Spanish-speaking environments.

Some patterns in the Spanish data reflect tendencies that are seen across the twenty-seven languages. For example, children learning Spanish and other languages acquire stop consonants such as *p*, *b*, *t*, *d*, *k*, and *g*, and nasal consonants like *m* and *n*, before sounds that require finer articulatory control, such as fricatives like *f* and *s*. Within the set of stop consonants, children acquire the voiceless stops *p*, *t*, and *k* before their voiced counterparts *b*, *d*, and *g*, which require a speaker to activate the vocal cords while forming the stop closure. They learn consonants produced with the lips before similar sounds produced farther back in the mouth: *p* before *t* and *k*, *b* before *d*, and *m* before *n* and *ñ*. This is probably because children can see labial sounds being pronounced as well as hearing them; in fact, blind children are less likely to favor these sounds (Pérez-Pereira and Conti-Ramsden 1999, 69–70). Finally, in Spanish and other languages that have the trilled *r* and/or the voiced bilabial fricative /β/ (as in *abajo* or *suave*), these are among the last sounds that children learn. Almost six percent of children are still working on the *r* in their "tween" years (Perelló Gilberga 2002, 284), and many children require speech therapy to master the trill.

Children learning Spanish are unusual, however, in their early acquisition of the palatal nasal *ñ* and the affricate *ch*. These are among the earliest sounds these children learn (Slide 5.4), while children learning other languages generally acquire them after many of the sounds that Spanish children learn later, namely *g, n, b, d, f,* and the /x/ of *ajo.* This is especially striking given that *ñ* and *ch* are among the least frequent consonants in Spanish (Guirao and García Jurado 1990). However, as shown in Slide 5.1, *ch* is a frequent substitute consonant in speech addressed to children, as in *chocho* for *sucio*; perhaps *ñ* is likewise more common in speech addressed to children.

Even before children learning Spanish begin to speak, they learn not to pay attention to sounds, and sound contrasts, that are not relevant in the language. (Likewise, Japanese babies quickly learn to ignore the contrast between *r* and *l* (Tsushima et al. 1994).) Thus while six-month-old babies learning Spanish (or English) pay attention to the difference between *b* and *v*, one-year-old babies learning Spanish have learned to "tune out" this difference (Slide 5.5, Pons et al. 2009). This is a useful fact to have at one's fingertips when encouraging students to avoid the English *v* sound when speaking Spanish.

### Teacher talk

"Tanto los niños hispanos como los niños en general aprenden primero las consonantes que son fáciles de pronunciar, como la *pe,* la *te* y la *ka,* mientras las consonantes más difíciles como la *erre* y la *ese* son las últimas a aprender. También, las consonantes producidas con los labios se aprenden antes de consonantes similares producidas más al fondo de la boca: *pe* antes de *te* y *ka, be* antes de *de* y *eme* antes de *ene* y *eñe.* La *erre* y la *be* suave de *amaba* son las consonantes más difíciles de aprender en español y en otros idiomas que tienen estos sonidos. Muchos niños todavía tienen dificultades con la *erre* cuando tienen más de diez años y necesitan ayuda profesional para aprenderla. Mientras aprenden los sonidos del español, los bebés hispanos aprenden a ignorar los sonidos que no existen en el idioma, como la *uve.*"

### In-class activity

- **Predict the order of acquisition of consonants.** Students consider a list of the consonants of Spanish (Slide 5.6) and predict which are learned at different ages. The instructor can then show Slide 5.4 for the correct answer. The class can discuss what makes a sound harder or easier to learn. Are the same sounds difficult for children and for English-speaking second-language learners of Spanish? Why is the trilled *r* such a common sound worldwide (Chapter 2) even though it is hard to learn?

### Take-home project

- **Observe a two-year-old's speech.** At home, students watch the first part of the video linked to in Slide 5.7, which features a two-year-old girl speaking Spanish. They take notes on the words she mispronounces, using the form embedded in that slide. For example, in the fourth segment, the girl pronounces *super bien* as *uper men*. Students then rewatch the video in class. Before playing each segment, the teacher asks students about words the girl mispronounced and writes these on the board; after listening to the segment, the class can confirm, modify, or reject these mispronunciations.

By the end of this exercise, the board will show a substantial list of agreed-on mispronunciations. If the class has already discussed the normal order of acquisition of consonants (Slide 5.4), students (perhaps working in groups) can now address the question of how the girl's mispronunciations do or do not reflect this order. For example, *uper men* for *super bien* reflects children's late acquisition of /s/ and /b/. Alternatively, this activity can serve as a springboard for presenting and discussing that slide.

This starts as a take-home project because students will find that they need to play some parts of the video more than once in order to hear and write down the girl's mispronunciations.

### First words

#### Just the facts

The first words of children learning Spanish concern their daily life: people, activities and interactions, animals and noises, toys, body parts, food and drink, and other objects children see every day. Slide 5.8 lists a few dozen typical early words, based on questionnaires filled out by parents of Mexican or Mexican-American children (Jackson-Maldonado et al. 1993). The words were reported to be actively used by sixty percent of the sixty-eight children in the study, aged 1;3 to 2;7.

Since children's early vocabularies are so small, it is natural for children to use their early words to express additional meanings. These overextensions are typically based on objects' shape or function. Slide 5.9 illustrates one toddler's prodigious overextensions (Macken 1978). This child used *manzana* to refer to all fruit as well as other round objects such as balls, eggs, and even some animals (perhaps because of their round eyes). *Guaguau* served for all animals. Finally, he used *agua* to refer to juice, water-related objects (cups, soap and bubbles, boats), and some blue and green objects (the sky, a green book).

#### Teacher talk

"Las primeras palabras de niños aprendiendo español como su primer idioma tienen que ver con su vida diaria: personas, actividades e interacciones, animales y ruidos, juguetes, partes del cuerpo, comidas y bebidas y otros objetos. Los niños pueden extender el uso de sus primeras palabras para referir a una variedad de objetos relacionados."

*In-class activities*

- **Predict children's first words**. Before showing Slide 5.8, the teacher asks pairs or groups of students to list some Spanish words they think children will learn first. Students can list individual words or group them into categories. These lists can then be compared with the actual words in the slide. Are they what the students expected? Why do children learn these words first?
- **Categorize children's first words**. In this activity, students look over a list of early words (Slide 5.10, which alphabetizes the words in Slide 5.8) and decide which semantic categories, such as foods or body parts, best describe them. Students can simply identify the categories or can take the additional step of assigning words to categories, either by listing words within each category or by labeling the words on a printed copy of the slide. Class discussion can revolve around the question of why these are the first words learned.
- **Analyze children's semantic overextensions**. As discussed above, Slide 5.9 shows one child's early overextensions of the words *manzana, guaguau,* and *agua*. Students discuss in pairs the logic behind these overextensions, then share their thoughts with the class. Can they think of similar examples from young children learning English?

### Learning semantic contrasts

*Just the facts*

Semantic contrasts such as *por* versus *para* and *ser* versus *estar* are doubly challenging for Spanish students. Not only are these contrasts lacking in English, but they are also complex, since these words express a wide and overlapping range of meanings. For example, both *por* and *para* can refer to time (*por la tarde, para el martes*), space (*por la calle, el tren para Madrid*), and purpose (*por dinero, para jugar*). *Ser* and *estar* can each designate location (*La fiesta es aquí, Aquí está tu camisa*) and qualities (*La camisa es roja y está mojada*).

Children use a divide-and-conquer strategy to acquire these complex contrasts. That is, at first they typically use each of them to express a single meaning, then add more meanings slowly (Slide 5.11, based on Bedore 1999; Castro Yánez and Sandoval Zúñiga 2009; Peronard 1985). The first uses of *por*, which is rarer than *para* in children's language, are invariably spatial, reflecting children's focus on spatial relationships in their play. Most children first use *para* for recipients (*para mí*) or purpose (*para jugar*), though some start with a spatial usage. Young children first use *estar* exclusively to express location, while using *ser* with a following noun. *Estar* then emerges as a present progressive auxiliary and both verbs begin to appear with adjectives. In general, children and parents alike use distinct sets of adjectives with these two verbs (Slide 5.12, based on Sera 1992), which helps prevent errors such as *\*La sopa es caliente* or *\*El tren está peligroso*, which one might hear in a second language classroom. Children do not learn the most sophisticated *ser/estar* difference – the use of *ser* to express the location of events – until their teenage years (Sera 1992).

### Teacher talk

"Los niños hispanos aprenden poco a poco la diferencia entre *por* y *para*, y también la diferencia entre *ser* y *estar*. Primero usan solo un sentido de cada palabra y añaden otros sentidos a lo largo de los meses y hasta años."

### In-class activities

- **Predict children's first uses of *por*, *para*, *ser*, and *estar*.** In this activity students work in pairs to predict which uses of *por* and *para*, and also *ser* and *estar*, children learn first. These might be the uses that students consider to be most basic or important overall, or, alternatively, uses that they expect children are most likely to hear in their daily lives. The instructor can use the list of uses in Slide 5.13 or his or her own list. Students should present and explain their predictions to the class. At this time, the instructor can show Slide 5.11 and the class can discuss why the uses shown are the first to emerge.
- **Contrast L1 and L2 learning of *por* and other prepositions.** The acquisition of *por* and other prepositions raises two interesting differences between first and second language learners of Spanish.
  - *First uses of* por. Like children (see above and Slide 5.14), second-language learners at first use *por* with limited meanings (Zuzik 2013). Unlike children, whose first uses are spatial, their first uses usually involve time or date (*por tres minutos*, *por dos semanas*), fixed expressions (e.g. *por favor*, *por ejemplo*), or both (*por la mañana*). In this activity teachers can present Slide 5.14 to students and ask them for possible explanations of this difference. Alternatively, teachers can ask students to predict which uses of *por* might be first for children and for second-language learners. The class can debate these predictions, then discuss how they compare with the actual pattern.
  - *Considering fear of prepositions.* Slide 5.15 shares a quotation from a teacher of advanced-level Spanish in Spain about his students' difficulties learning prepositions and the strategies they use to avoid using prepositions they are unsure of (Silverio 1997, 382). Children,

in contrast, are less inhibited and freely make mistakes. In this activity, the class should read the quotation and discuss their reaction to it. Do they find themselves adopting these avoidance strategies, for prepositions and/or other domains of Spanish? What is the worst thing that could happen if they used the wrong preposition when speaking Spanish? The same quotation could be a jumping-off point for an in-class or at-home writing assignment about the emotional side of language learning.

### Noun agreement

*Just the facts*

Gender agreement is one of the most challenging aspects of Spanish for English-speaking second-language learners. English lacks gender agreement but it is ubiquitous in Spanish, affecting adjectives, articles, and pronouns in almost every Spanish sentence. This very ubiquity may explain why Spanish children master gender agreement early: by age three or earlier (Mariscal 2008).

Children master gender agreement in three steps. In the first, they use masculine and feminine forms without any apparent awareness of grammatical gender. These forms may fluctuate; for example, one child sometimes described an *enanito* as *bueno* and *\*buena* at different times, and another described a *campana* as either *\*roto* or *rota*. Or children may use each adjective in a single form that reflects its most common context in family discourse: for example, *fría* and *mala*, learned in the context of *agua fría* and *bruja mala*.

In the second step, children extract the basic *-o/-a* pattern of gender agreement and apply it correctly to regular nouns like *libro* and *casa* as well as words with obvious gender such as *madre* and *padre*. From this point on, they rarely produce incorrect sentences such as *\*La casa es rojo* or *\*Es un madre*, as second language learners so often do. (The same is true for adults, as discussed in "Speech errors" later in this chapter). However, at this stage children occasionally make mistakes on words that do not end in *-o* or *-a* or have irregular gender (e.g. *la moto*), altering either nouns or their modifiers to enforce the *-o/-a* pattern (Slide 5.16, based on Clark 1985; Mariscal 2008; Pérez-Pereira 1991). These are analogous to children's errors learning English, such as *\*mouses* for *mice* and *\*eated* for *ate*. In the final step of acquisition children eliminate such errors.

Children learn number agreement at a young age as well (Marrero and Aguirre 2003). In fact, their first unambiguous plurals appear before they can reliably pronounce a final *-s* sound. At this stage children can already mark plurals with the definite article *los*, often reduced to *lo* or even *o*, as in *o huevo* for *los huevos*. Another early sign of number agreement is a final *-e* in words like *pece* (for *peces*), *luce* (*luces*), and *balone* (*balones*).

*Teacher talk*

"Los niños hispanos aprenden fácilmente la diferencia entre palabras masculinas y femeninas, antes de cumplir tres años. Los errores que cometen durante este proceso demuestran que han aprendido la regla española básica de -*o* masculina y -*a* femenina."

*In-class activities*

- **Think about gender acquisition.** The contrast between first and second language acquisition of gender agreement is dramatic: children learn agreement quickly, but even advanced second-language learners continue to make agreement mistakes. This topic deserves a class discussion. Why do students find gender agreement difficult? Why do they think children learn it quickly? How can second-language learners be more like children? As noted above, the very ubiquity of gender may help children learn, especially since most of their early words are nouns.
- **Analyze children's gender errors.** The errors shown in Slide 5.16 demonstrate that once children learn that masculine and feminine words end in -*o* and -*a*, respectively, they overapply this rule to words that violate this generalization. In this activity, pairs of students work together to analyze these data, looking for patterns in the errors. There are three to be found, as color-coded in Slide 5.17: children either "correct" a final -*o* or -*a* that contradicts a word's gender, use an -*o* or -*a* to more clearly mark the gender of a word, or reinterpret a word's gender based on its ending. The teacher can either tell students there are three patterns to find or can leave the task more open-ended.

  Students may be interested in learning that these error patterns have parallels in the history of Spanish (Slide 5.18). The -*us* ending of Latin *socrus* and *nurus*, which was more often found in masculine words, was changed in Spanish to the more obviously feminine -*a* of *suegra* and *nuera*. The uninformative -*e* ending of Latin *passare*, *infante*, and *seniore* was changed in Spanish to an unambiguous -*o* or -*a* in *pájaro*, *infanta*, and *señora*. Finally, Latin's feminine noun *praefatio* was reassigned to the masculine gender in Spanish *prefacio* because of its final *o*. These are just a few examples.

## Order of acquisition of verb tenses

*Just the facts*

Children generally learn Spanish verb tenses in the order shown in Slide 5.19 (based on Bedore 1999; Blake 1985; Gathercole, Sebastián, and Soto 1999; Rojas Nieto 2003). The first tenses learned are the ones that are most relevant to children's conversations: they express what is happening (*El tren entra en el túnel, El bebé está durmiendo*), what has happened (*Se cayó, ¿Dónde has puesto el gato?*), and what parents (and other interlocutors) want children to do (*Cómelo*). These functions take priority even though some of the tenses involved, namely the present indicative, the preterite, and the imperative, are harder to conjugate than the imperfect and the immediate *ir a* future, which are learned later, not to mention the conjugated future and the conditional, which are rarely even mentioned in studies of children's acquisition of Spanish.

Slide 5.19 also shows a clear interaction between dialect and language acquisition. In Spain, where speakers use the present perfect to talk about recent events, thus somewhat displacing the preterite ("Variation in verb use," in Chapter 4), it is one of the first tenses children learn. In Latin America, where the present perfect is less frequent, it is learned more than a year later.

A click on the slide gives more details about stages in the acquisition of the imperative and the subjunctive. It is not surprising that affirmative commands are learned before negative commands, since their conjugation is more familiar (e.g. *habla* versus *no hables*). Children first use the subjunctive in noun clauses after verbs of volition, and also in certain adverbial clauses, especially with *para que*. These uses are followed closely by adjective clauses. Blake (1985) points out that these early contexts all refer to future events or descriptions. It takes children several additional years to learn to use the subjunctive in noun clauses after expressions of doubt, possibility, or emotion. In fact, Blake presents evidence that adults in both Mexico and Spain do not always use the subjunctive in these contexts, a variability that must impede children's learning.

### Teacher talk

"Los niños hispanos aprenden primero los tiempos verbales que son más relevantes a sus vidas y conversaciones: los tiempos que describen lo que pasa, lo que ha pasado y lo que otras personas quieren que pase. Los niños expresan estas funciones primero aunque unas de las conjugaciones necesarias, como el presente y el pretérito, son más difíciles que unas conjugaciones que aprenden más tarde, como el imperfecto."

### In-class activities

*   **Spot tenses in videos of children speaking Spanish**. This activity introduces the topic of verb acquisition and is also entertaining. The teacher plays one or more videos of young Hispanic children talking (Slide 5.20). Students take notes on the verb forms they hear. What tenses do these children use and not use?

- **Analyze the order of acquisition of verb tenses.** Students work in small groups to analyze the order of acquisition shown in Slide 5.19. This can be done first for the main table, and then for the smaller boxes that show stages of acquisition for commands and the subjunctive. In each analysis, students form hypotheses about why the tenses are learned in the order shown. The class then discusses these hypotheses as a group.

  The class can also compare children's order of acquisition of tenses (including uses of the subjunctive) with the order used in their textbook, or that they remember following in earlier classes. In what ways is it the same or different? How important or logical is it for a second language course to reflect children's natural course of language development?

### Learning to conjugate

*Just the facts*

The Spanish verb system boasts three conjugation classes, over a dozen tenses, six verb forms per conjugation, and dozens of irregular verbs. Learning to conjugate verbs is therefore a genuine challenge for Hispanic children as well as Spanish students, a process that takes more than four years (Bedore 1999). Children's learning of verb conjugations follows a developmental pathway that is similar to their acquisition of gender, described above. Children first learn unanalyzed verb forms. Next, they extract conjugation rules, which they apply to regular verbs and overapply to irregular verbs. Finally, they clean up the irregulars.

In the first stage of acquisition, children usually use one form of each verb: typically, the form they hear most. Consider, for example, the case study of a Mexican girl shown in Slide 5.21 (based on Rojas Nieto 2003). This girl's first verb forms reflect the reality of her daily activities. For example, the imperative *Mira* calls someone's attention, present-tense *cabe* describes how toys or other objects fit together, and past-tense *cayó* announces that something fell, a common occurrence in the playroom. For the same reason, the child's mother also used most of these verbs in the same single forms, as shown by the check marks (✓) in the slide. Although many of these early verb forms were irregular (*ven, ten, quiero, puedo, hay, sirve,* and *hizo*), at this point, the girl had no way of knowing this. She had learned them by rote.

In the second stage, children observe and begin to apply verb conjugation patterns. New patterns are not learned across-the-board but rather piecemeal, to use Gathercole, Sebastian, and Soto's terminology (1999), as children add new forms to verbs previously used in a single form. A verb's second form might add a contrast of person, number, tense, or mood (Slide 5.22, based on Rojas Nieto 2003). This is very different from the typical learning pattern in the Spanish language classroom, in which students learn one verb tense at a time and practice it with all the verbs they know.

When children successfully extract conjugation rules from contrasts such as those in Slide 5.22, this new knowledge shows not only in their correct conjugations of additional verbs, but also in their "corrections" of irregular verbs, resulting in forms such as *sabo for sé (Slide 5.23, based on Gathercole, Sebastian, and Soto 1999, Clark 1985, and Bedore 1999). These errors are common in the Spanish language classroom as well, and children learning English make similar mistakes, such as *eated for ate and *falled for fell. The slide also shows examples of other familiar error types: overuse of -ar endings (e.g. *saló for salió) and overextension of stem changes (e.g. *juegar for jugar) or the g of the -go ending (e.g. *pongar). In the third stage, children gradually eliminate these errors.

As with noun gender, many of children's errors parallel historical changes in Spanish (Slide 5.24). Over time Spanish speakers have regularized irregular verbs, added to the -ar conjugation class, and extended common irregular patterns.

## Teacher talk

"Los niños hispanos aprenden las conjugaciones verbales poco a poco. Primero aprenden formas individuales comunes como ¡Mira! o Cayó sin saber analizarlas. Cuando adquieren más formas empiezan a prestar atención a las conjugaciones y extraen las reglas. Entonces aplican las reglas a verbos regulares y también irregulares, así cometiendo unos de los mismos errores que se oyen en la clase de español como *sabo por sé o *juga por juega. Siguen eliminando estos errores hasta la edad de cinco años."

## In-class activity

* **Analyze children's conjugation errors**. Pairs or groups of students work with the list of errors shown in Slide 5.25, attempting to categorize the types of errors involved. (This could also be done as a take-home assignment.) Students then present and explain their results. The teacher can then show the categories in Slide 5.23 for comparison.
* **Think about the verb acquisition process.** Given how much effort Spanish students put into learning verb conjugations, the topic of how children learn these same rules should be of great interest. The class can discuss this topic either after the previous activity or in conjunction with Slides 5.21–5.23. Some possible questions to address, according to class interest, are the following:
  ◦ What verb conjugation mistakes do children make when learning English that are analogous to those made by children learning Spanish?

○ The traditional Spanish second-language student learns verb conjugations by a process very different from the one described above. Students receive explicit instruction, whereas children figure out conjugations for themselves. Students learn one conjugation at a time, and practice it for all the verbs they know, whereas children learn conjugations piecemeal. Should Spanish teachers try to teach conjugations in a way that mimics children's learning? Or are the circumstances of first- and second-language learning so different that it makes sense for each group to learn in a different fashion?

○ When children learn conjugation rules, they begin to make mistakes on irregular verb forms that they may have produced correctly in the past. In other words, progress in acquisition produces a temporary regression in performance. Does this happen in any other type of learning, or is it unique to learning languages?

### Take-home project

• **Ask a native speaker about children's conjugation errors.** This activity requires students to work with a native speaker partner as described in the Introduction. Each student should ask their partner how children learn to conjugate verbs in Spanish. What are the first verb forms children learn? How do children figure out the conjugation patterns? What kinds of mistakes do they make? Giving *sabo as an example of a typical error should be helpful. Students can summarize their findings in a written, oral, or graphic report.

### Second-language learning

### Just the facts

Learning Spanish as a second language is both similar to and different from learning Spanish from birth. On the one hand, all learners face the genuine challenges of Spanish, such as its trilled *r* and irregular verbs, and so are apt to make the same mistakes: for example, substituting an easier sound for the *r* and *sabo for *sé*. On the other hand, second-language learners have several disadvantages. First and foremost, while children learn their first language using the brain's left hemisphere, which is evolutionarily adapted for this task, later learners must rely on general-purpose learning mechanisms (Werker and Tees 2005). Second, later learners suffer from interference from their first language. For example, grammatical gender, which children easily master, is notoriously problematic for speakers of languages like English, which lacks this concept. Finally, situational aspects of learning further hamper second-language learners. Most have limited exposure to Spanish, and many find themselves nervous and/or apprehensive in a second-language classroom, whereas children are fully immersed in Spanish within a (usually) supportive family environment.

This limited exposure makes it particularly difficult for second language learners to develop adequate listening comprehension skills. While children hear Spanish from birth, language pedagogy traditionally emphasizes speaking, writing, and reading at the expense of listening. Moreover, listening is hard: spoken Spanish can be quite fast, and the listener cannot normally stop to look up words or to "rewind" a conversation. The result is that while children's listening comprehension skills typically outpace their speaking, the opposite is generally true for second-language learners. Many attain a reasonable degree of speaking proficiency but still find it difficult to understand spoken Spanish, especially "normal" Spanish that is not adapted for a second-language listener.

The activities in this section invite the second-language learner to step outside the learning process via reflection and experimentation. In addition, in-class activities for most of the first-language acquisition topics discussed earlier in the chapter invite students to compare children's experience learning Spanish with their own.

*Teacher talk*

"En ciertos respectos, aprender el español es un proceso similar para los niños y los estudiantes de español. Los dos grupos tienen que dominar aspectos difíciles del idioma, como la *erre* y los verbos irregulares, por lo tanto cometen errores parecidos, tal vez sustituyendo la *erre* por un sonido más fácil por y diciendo *sabo* por *sé*. Pero desafortunadamente los estudiantes de español tienen que aprender sin la gran ventaja de la juventud, y sufren de interferencia de su primer idioma. También tienen menos horas de contacto con el idioma, y en un contexto menos íntimo. Es por eso que sus esfuerzos son tan importantes."

*In-class activities*

- **Reflect on second language learning.** As mentioned above, several activities earlier in this chapter, such as "Think about gender acquisition" and "Analyze the order of acquisition of verb tenses," encourage students to reflect on their experiences learning specific aspects of Spanish. Reflecting on the learning process can be valuable more generally. For example, when approaching a new list of vocabulary words, student pairs or groups can discuss the different techniques they use to memorize vocabulary, such as inventing mnemonics for non-cognates. The pairs or groups can then share their preferred techniques (and/or mnemonics) with the class.

- **Brainstorm on applications of learning styles.** The "Visual, Auditory, Reading/Writing, Kinesthetic" characterization of learning styles can be a useful framework for class discussion, especially when applied to specific learning tasks (Fleming and Baume 2006). Slide 5.26 illustrates these learning styles as applied to the words *arriba* and *abajo*. A visual learner might associate the words with images related to the concepts of 'up' and 'down.' An auditory learner might sing the words with high and low notes, respectively. A learner who depends on the written word might focus on the relationships between words, whether coincidental (*arriba* and *árbol*) or actual (*abajo* and *bajo*). A kinesthetic learner might reach up while practicing *arriba* and crouch down for *bajo*.

  There are two basic ways to organize a brainstorming activity focused on learning styles. Most simply, student groups can each attempt to apply the four learning styles to a given topic, such as directional adverbs. To make the activity more personally relevant, the class can instead break into four groups, according to each student's preferred learning style. (These can be subdivided into smaller groups if necessary, and uncertain students can join whichever group needs more students.) Each group brainstorms ways to apply their learning style to the topic. At that point, each group can share their results with the class – or, using a "jigsaw" structure, the class can reform into groups that include a representative of each learning style. Each student in the new group describes one or more applications of their original group's learning style; the new group discusses these, chooses their favorite, and presents it to the class along with their reasoning.

- **Self-profile the student as a language learner.** This is an ongoing activity. Each time the class pauses to reflect on language learning, students add to a list or journal to keep track of how they learn best. This could culminate in a poster presentation at the end of the course.

*Take-home project*

- **Try a sample online Spanish lesson.** Today's Spanish students have access to an enormous variety of Spanish-learning resources, from paid programs to free websites. In this activity, each student picks one such resource, tries a sample lesson, and shares the results. Students can choose a resource listed in one of the sources in Slide 5.27 or find one on their own. Teachers may want to ensure that each student picks a different resource, and/or have students explain their choices before embarking on a sample lesson. Students will certainly need some guidance for how much of an effort to make. The teacher may ask them to spend some minimum number of minutes, or to complete a single lesson as defined by the specific program.

Afterward, students should report to the class on their experience. What did they learn about Spanish and/or the learning process? How did the methodology compare with their experience in the Spanish classroom? What did they like or dislike? Would they recommend the program?

• **Tackle listening comprehension.** Like the Chapter 2 project "Tackle the trilled *r*," this project challenges students to improve a specific skill that eludes many learners. As a first step, the class agrees on a significant but feasible time commitment, perhaps listening to Spanish fifteen minutes a day for two weeks. Each student then identifies a listening resource, or combination of resources, that they will enjoy, and justifies their choice after a sample listening session. (The list of "Absorption Materials" at https://www.reddit.com/r/Spanish/wiki/resources is a good place to start.) On the basis of this sample session, students also agree on a listening protocol. For example, should they listen to each selection only once, or repeat it? Should they listen straight through, or replay parts that they do not understand?

For a subjective assessment of this project, students can log their daily listening along with a brief reflection, perhaps combined with an overall reflection at the end of the project. For an objective assessment, the teacher can administer in-class listening clozes at the beginning and end of the project. Any change in cloze scores can inform students' reflections whether or not it figures into their grades.

## Using Spanish

### Speech errors

*Just the facts*

Just as physicians learn from autopsies, physicists from particle collisions, and transportation engineers from plane crashes, linguists learn from the spontaneous errors made by proficient speakers of Spanish and other languages. These errors are a surprising and fascinating source of evidence for how the mind produces and organizes language. The discussion here is based on research by del Viso (2002), Hoyos Arvizu (2009), and Mendizábal de la Cruz (2004).

Errors in which Spanish speakers unintentionally interchange words reveal how they plan and execute sentences. As shown in Slide 5.28, these errors typically involve words that are several words apart, or even in different clauses. This shows that speakers subconsciously plan ahead as they speak, having an entire sentence in mind before speaking. These errors also show that gender and number agreement is the final step in Spanish speech production, after the words have been "filled in," so to speak. Notice that in the first sentence the articles *esos* and *la* agree with the erroneous nouns *coches* and *rueda*, not the planned nouns *ruedas* and *coche*. Likewise, in the second sentence *este* and *una* agree with erroneous *atasco* and *lluvia*. In the third sentence, *el* and *acerque* both agree with *fuego*, not the intended *niños*.

Errors in which Spanish speakers mistakenly use the wrong word reveal the multiple ways they mentally organize their vocabulary: by sound, by meaning, and by part of speech. As shown in Slide 5.29, word substitutions are not random. Substituted words either sound similar to intended words, for example *concursos* for *recursos*, or are semantically related, as in *ciegos* for *sordos*. And in every case, nouns replace nouns, adjectives replace adjectives, and verbs replace verbs, showing that speakers subconsciously know a word's part of speech. Likewise, all the interchange errors in Slide 5.28 are noun-for-noun.

Errors that involve only parts of words reveal that speakers subconsciously know how to divide words into syllables (Slide 5.30). The entire syllable *me* is lost in the first example, and *lla* is added in the second. The interchanges in examples 3 and 4 affect consonants that begin or end similar syllables, while those in examples 5 and 6 involve multiple syllables. These errors are particularly intriguing because even educated speakers are only marginally aware of syllables, especially now that word processing software hyphenates words automatically.

### Teacher talk

"No solo los estudiantes de español sino también los hispanohablantes nativos cometen errores cuando hablan español. Estos errores nos dan un vistazo a cómo la mente humana organiza y produce el lenguaje. Por ejemplo, cuando se usa una palabra incorrecta, suele ser una palabra parecida a la original, en sonido o sentido, y siempre de la misma categoría gramatical, como nombre o verbo. Esto muestra que un ser humano organiza su vocabulario según múltiples aspectos de las palabras."

### In-class activity

- **Interpret speech errors.** This would be a good activity to introduce this topic. Students work in pairs or groups to interpret the speech errors shown in Slide 5.31. They try to deduce what the speakers intended to say and identify what went wrong. The teacher can then click on the slide to show the intended utterances (in the thought bubbles).

*Take-home project*

• **Compare Spooner and Pich i Pon.** This is a historical research project for
an individual student (or pair of students) to carry out and share with
the class. Reverend William Archibald Spooner, an Oxford don, and
Joan Pich i Pon, a Catalan politician, were both notorious for their slips
of the tongue, sometimes called *spoonerisms* in English and *piquipona-
das* in Spanish. Whereas Spooner typically erred by transposing ("me-
tathesizing") two sounds, as in *You have hissed all my mystery lectures*,
Pich i Pon was more likely to use the wrong word, as in *Es que ahora
hago una vida sedimentaria* (instead of *sedentaria*).

  The student who takes on this project should learn about the two people
and the mistakes they are famous for. He or she should describe to the class
who they were, and present and compare examples of their errors. The student should also address the veracity of these errors. Did Spooner and Pich
i Pon actually commit the errors, or were they merely attributed to them? If
they were genuine, were they spontaneous or planned?

## Language and thought

*Just the facts*

Can speaking Spanish affect the way people think? Laboratory studies on
two aspects of Spanish grammar suggest that the answer is "yes."

  First, grammatical gender appears to affect the way Spanish speakers
think about inanimate objects. Boroditsky, Schmidt, and Phillips (2003)
asked Spanish and German speakers to describe in English (their second
language) several objects that have different gender in these two languages
(Slide 5.32). Spanish speakers used dainty adjectives such as *golden, intricate,*
and *little* to describe objects that are feminine in Spanish (such as *llave* 'key')
and virile adjectives such as *big, dangerous,* and *long* to describe objects that
are masculine (e.g. *puente* 'bridge'). The German speakers chose very different adjectives, such as *hard, heavy,* and *jagged* for masculine *Schlüssel* 'key'
and *beautiful, elegant,* and *fragile* for feminine *Brücke* 'bridge.' Also, when
asked to memorize personal names for inanimate objects, such as an apple
named "Patrick," speakers recalled these names better if they conformed to
the objects' grammatical gender in their native language.

  Second, the "*se accidental*" structure (as in *Se me rompió la taza*), which
de-emphasizes the person who causes an accident, apparently makes Spanish
speakers less likely to remember such individuals. Fausey and Boroditsky
(2011) showed videos of deliberate and accidental events to speakers of
English and Spanish (Slide 5.33). Afterward, English speakers were equally
likely to remember who caused both types of events, but Spanish speakers were less likely to remember who caused the accidents: a modest but

statistically significant difference. Fausey et al. (2010) found a similar effect when they compared speakers of English and Japanese, which has a structure similar to the *se accidental*.

## Teacher talk

"Según unos experimentos interesantes, el español afecta el pensamiento de sus hablantes. Primero, se ha notado que de modo subconsciente, los hispanohablantes asignan características masculinas y femeninas a los objetos según su género gramatical, por ejemplo describiendo una llave como *lovely* y un puente como *sturdy*. El '*se* accidental', una estructura que evita mencionar a la persona que causó un accidente, también afecta el pensamiento. Después de ver videos de eventos intencionados o accidentales, los hispanohablantes no se acuerdan de las personas que causaron los accidentes tanto como las que causaron los eventos intencionados, una diferencia que no muestran los angloparlantes."

## Take-home projects

- **Reproduce a grammatical gender experiment.** Students can carry out a simplified version of Boroditsky, Schmidt, and Phillips's experiment on memory and grammatical gender (2003). Students will need to prepare stimulus cards that each show a picture of an inanimate object paired with a masculine or feminine personal name (in English), such as an apple and the name *Harry*. Half the objects should be grammatically masculine in Spanish, and half feminine; half the objects of each gender should be paired with names that match their gender, and half with names that clash. Slide 5.34 shows one sample setup for this experiment, with gender-matching objects and names shaded in yellow. The student investigators will need another set of test cards that show the objects without their assigned names. (For a controlled experiment, different test subjects should see different combinations of objects and names just in case some pairings happen to be easier to memorize. For this reason, every name in the setup has an opposite-gender counterpart, such as *Claudia* for *Claude* and *Donald* for *Donna*.)

  Test subjects should be a combination of monolingual English speakers and native Spanish speakers, who may or may not speak English. The student investigator should first show all the stimulus cards to each test subject, perhaps for five seconds per card, then show them the (randomized) test cards and ask them to supply the missing names. Ideally, the results will echo those of Boroditsky, Schmidt, and Phillips, with Spanish speakers more accurately remembering names that match their objects' grammatical gender but English speakers not showing this difference.

- **Find a meme for the *se accidental*.** Using search terms such as *se me*, *se lo*, and *se nos*, students find online memes that use the *se accidental*, such as the one linked to in Slide 5.35. They save these to a shared location online, perhaps as separate slides in a Google Slides presentation, so that they can be shared and enjoyed in class. No duplicates!

   As an alternative, students can use one of the "meme generators" available online to create their own *se accidental* memes.

### Spanish "Pig Latin"

*Just the facts*

Language games, as linguists call pastimes like Pig Latin, are another surprising source of evidence for speakers' implicit knowledge of their native language. In particular, Spanish language games, called *jerigonzas*, reveal speakers' knowledge of word and syllable structure. As noted in the section above on speech errors, such a finding is particularly intriguing because this knowledge is highly implicit: only a poet or a typesetter actually thinks about syllables. Nevertheless, most Spanish speakers are able to successfully manipulate words, sounds, and syllables in the context of a language game.

For any *jerigonza*, speakers must divide a word into syllables. This alone is an intellectual feat. For example, as shown in Slide 5.36, speakers divide *canción* into two syllables, and *maestro* and *pájaro* each into three. In other words, they implicitly know that *cion* constitutes a single syllable, but *maes* constitutes two: a sophisticated distinction that most Spanish learners never master. Speakers then insert a nonsense syllable, like *cha* or *pa*, either before, after, or within each syllable. The slide illustrates all three possibilities (Piñeros 1998, 61). *Cha* precedes each syllable in the Peruvian *jerigonza*, while *pa* follows each syllable in the Colombian variety, with its vowel changing to reflect the main vowel of each syllable (*e* for *pe*, and *o* for *cion*, *tro*, and *ro*). The Costa Rican *jerigonza* requires the greatest degree of linguistic skill, with *pa*, *pe*, or *po* inserted mid-syllable, before any syllable-final consonant. In other words, the speaker must not only divide each word into syllables, but also surgically subdivide complex syllables.

*Teacher talk*

"Las diferentes versiones de Pig Latin en español, que se llaman *jerigonzas*, son evidencia de la gran capacidad lingüística de hispanohablantes. Los hablantes tienen que dividir cada palabra en sílabas y añadir una nueva sílaba como *cha* o *pa*. Es difícil hacerlo rápido pero con práctica se puede lograrlo."

*In-class activity*

- **Practice a *jerigonza*.** The teacher (or class) chooses one of the *jerigonzas* from slide 5.36, guides the class through some sample words, then gives student pairs time to practice it. This activity has several possible variations:
  ◦ *Jerigonza.* Student pairs can all practice the same *jerigonza*, or each pair can pick one.
  ◦ *Material.* The teacher can give students a list of words to practice, or a sample paragraph. Or students can try reading any passage from their textbook (or other source) or have a free-form conversation.
  ◦ *Performance.* After students have practiced, the teacher can ask some of them (as *víctimas o voluntarios*) to speak in *jerigonza* in front of the class.
  ◦ *Reflection.* The class can discuss what it felt like to speak in *jerigonza*. What were the challenges?

*Take-home projects*

- **Prepare a *jerigonza* dialogue.** Each pair of students practices a dialogue at home that they either videorecord or perform live in front of the class.
- **Ask a native speaker about *jerigonzas*.** This activity requires students to work with a native speaker partner as described in the Introduction. Each student asks their native speaker partner to describe *jerigonzas* they are familiar with. Perhaps they could record their partner saying a few sentences in *jerigonza*. Students can summarize their findings in a written, oral, or graphic report.

The following references are cited in this chapter's text and/or its accompanying PowerPoint presentation.

# References

Bedore, L. 1999. The acquisition of Spanish. In *Language acquisition across North America: Cross-cultural and cross-linguistic perspectives*, eds. O. Taylor and L. Leonard, 157–208. San Diego, CA: Singular.

Blake, R. 1985. From research to the classroom: Notes on the subjunctive. *Hispania* 68: 166–73.

Boroditsky, L., and L. A. Schmidt. 2000. Sex, syntax, and semantics. *Proceedings of the Annual Meeting of the Cognitive Science Society* 22: 42–47.

Boroditsky, L., L. A. Schmidt, and W. Phillips. 2003. Sex, syntax, and semantics. In *Language in mind: Advances in the study of language and thought*, eds. D. Getner and S. Goldin-Meadow, 61–89. Cambridge, MA: MIT Press.

Castro Yánez, G., and M. S. Sandoval Zúñiga. 2009. La aparición de las preposiciones en niños hispanohablantes entre los 18 y los 36 meses de edad. *Revista Latinoamericana de Psicología* 41: 243–54.

Clark, E. V. 1985. The acquisition of Romance. In *The crosslinguistic study of language acquisition. Vol. 1: The data*, ed. D. I. Slobin, 687–782. Hillsdale, NJ: Lawrence Erlbaum.

del Viso, S. 2002. Los *lapsus linguæ* como fuente de datos en el estudio de la producción del lenguaje: un *corpus* de errores en castellano. *Anuario de Psicología* 33: 355–84.

Fausey, C. M., and L. Boroditsky. 2011. Whodunnit? Cross-linguistic differences in eye-witness memory. *Psychonomic Bulletin & Review* 18: 150–57.

Fausey, C. M., B. L. Long, A. Inamori, and L. Boroditsky. 2010. Constructing agency: The role of language. *Frontiers in Cultural Psychology* 1(162): 1–11.

Ferguson, C. A. 1964. Baby talk in six languages. *American Anthropologist* 66: 103–14.

———. 1978. Talking to children: A search for universals. In *Method and Theory*. Vol. 1 of *Universals of human language*, eds. H. J. Greenberg, C. E. Ferguson, and E. A. Moravcsik, 203–24. Stanford, CA: Stanford University Press.

Fleming, N., and D. Baume. 2006. Learning styles again: VARKing up the right tree! *Educational Developments* 7(4) (November): 4–7.

Gathercole, V. C. M., E. Sebastián, and P. Soto. 1999. The early acquisition of Spanish verbal morphology: Across-the-board or piecemeal knowledge? *The International Journal of Bilingualism* 3: 133–82.

Guirao, M., and M. A. García Jurado. 1990. Frequency of occurence of phonemes in American Spanish. *Revue québécoise de linguistique* 19(2): 135–49.

Hochberg, J. 2016. *¿Por qué? 101 Questions about Spanish*. London: Bloomsbury.

Hoyos Arvizu, A. 2009. *Errores de habla y procesamiento de la producción: Una perspectiva lingüística*. PhD diss., Universidad Nacional de Educación a Distancia.

Jackson-Maldonado, D., D. Thal, V. Marchman, E. Bates, and V. Gutierrez-Clennen. 1993. Early lexical development in Spanish-speaking infants and toddlers. *Journal of Child Language* 20: 523–49.

Macken, M. 1978. Permitted complexity in phonological development: One child's acquisition of Spanish consonants. *Lingua* 44: 219–53.

Mariscal, S. 2008. Early acquisition of gender agreement in the Spanish noun phrase: Starting small. *Journal of Child Language* 35: 1–29.

Marrero, V., and C. Aguirre. 2003. Plural acquisition and development in Spanish. *Linguistic theory and language development in Hispanic languages*, eds. S. Montrul and F. Ordóñez, 275–96. Somerville, MA: Cascadilla Press.

McLeod, S., and K. Crowe, K. 2018. Children's consonant acquisition in 27 languages: A cross-linguistic review. *American Journal of Speech-Language Pathology* 27: 1546–71.

Mendizábal de la Cruz, N. 2004. Los errores espontáneos de la producción lingüística. *Artifara* 4. http://www.cisi.unito.it/artifara/rivista4/testi/errores.asp.

Penny, R. 2002. *A history of the Spanish language*. 2nd ed. Cambridge: Cambridge University Press.

Perelló Gilberga, J. 2002. *Trastornos del habla*. 5th ed. Barcelona: Masson.

Pérez-Pereira, M. 1991. The acquisition of gender: What Spanish children tell us. *Journal of Child Language* 18: 571–90.

Pérez-Pereira, M., and G. Conti-Ramsden. 1999. *Language development and social interaction in blind children*. Essays in developmental psychology. Hove: Psychology Press.

Peronard, M. 1985. Spanish prepositions introducing adverbial constructions. *Journal of Child Language* 12: 95–108.

Piñeros, C-E. 1998. *Prosodic morphology in Spanish: Constraint interaction in word-formation.* PhD diss., Ohio State University.

Pons, F., D. J. Lewkowicz, S. Soto-Faraco, and N. Sebastián-Gallés. 2009. Narrowing of intersensory speech perception in infancy. *PNAS* 106: 10598–602.

Rojas Nieto, C. 2003. Early acquisition of Spanish verb inflexion: A usage-based account. *Psychology of Language and Communication* 7: 17–36.

Sachs, J. 1979. The adaptive significance of linguistic input to prelinguistic infants. In *Talking to children: Language input and acquisition*, eds. C. E. Snow and C. A. Ferguson, 51–62. Cambridge: Cambridge University Press.

Sera, M. D. 1992. To be or not to be: Use and acquisition of the Spanish copulas. *Journal of Memory and Language* 31: 408–27.

Silverio, I. G. 1997. Adquisición y uso correcto de las preposiciones *a, en, para* y *por* en niveles superiores. In *El español como lengua extranjera: Del pasado al futuro*, eds. F. Moreno Fernández, M. Gil Bürmann, and K. Alonso, 380–86. Madrid: Universidad de Alcalá. http://cvc.cervantes.es/ensenanza/biblioteca_ele/asele/pdf/08/08_0377.pdf.

Tsushima, T., O. Takizawa, M. Sasaki, S. Siraki, K. Nishi, M. Kohno, P. Menyuk, and C. Best. 1994. Discrimination of English /r-l/ and /w-y/ by Japanese infants at 6–12 months: Language specific developmental changes in speech perception abilities. Paper presented at the International Conference on Spoken Language Processing, Yokohama, Japan.

Werker, J. F., and R. C. Tees. 2005. Speech perception as a window for understanding plasticity and commitment in language systems of the brain. *Developmental Psychobiology* 46: 233–51.

Zyzik, E. 2013. Functional approaches to second language Spanish. In *The handbook of Spanish second language acquisition*, ed. K. L. Geeslin, 30–45. Hoboken, NJ: Wiley-Blackwell.

# Appendix A

# In-class activities

This appendix characterizes this book's 128 in-class activities by their type (as listed in Table 2 in the Introduction) and appropriate level of Spanish. The activities "Discuss the language controversy in Catalonian schools" and "Contrast first and second language learners" are marked as both Read/ discuss and See/discuss because the discussion can be based either on a text extract or an image. Many activities are appropriate for more than one level of Spanish, either because they are feasible and interesting for all levels "as is," or because teachers can adapt them, as discussed in the Introduction.

Also as described in the Introduction, activities in boldface are of sufficient interest that teachers should consider using them in their classes even if they do not adopt the book's essential questions curriculum more broadly.

Activities marked with an asterisk (*) can be done as take-home projects instead of in class. Activities marked with a double asterisk (**) correspond to take-home projects that supplement or replace them.

| | Type of activity | | | | | | | | | | | Spanish level | | |
|---|---|---|---|---|---|---|---|---|---|---|---|---|---|---|
| | Activate knowledge | Analyze | Debate | Discuss | Create | Listen | Practice | Categorize | Read/discuss | See/discuss | Watch/discuss | Beginning | Intermediate | Advanced |
| *Chapter 1* | | | | | | | | | | | | | | |
| Rank Spanish among the world's top languages | × | | | | | | | | | | | × | × | × |
| **Rank the top five Spanish-speaking countries** | × | | | | | | | | | | | × | × | × |
| Map Spanish-speaking countries by name and population size | | | | | × | | | | | | | × | | |
| Learn from videos about the Real Academia Española | | | | | | | | | | | × | | × | × |
| Debate the Real Academia Española | | | × | | | | | | | | | | | × |
| Discuss the elimination of ch and ll | | | | | | | | | × | | | | | × |
| Map the origins of Nobel Prize winners | | | | | × | | | | | | | × | | |
| **Pick a favorite Nobel Prize winner** | | | | | | | | | | | | | × | × |
| A design project for the inverted marks | | | | | × | | | | | | | × | | × |
| **Explore the history of the inverted marks** | | | | | | | | | | × | | | × | × |
| Debate the inverted marks | | | × | | | | | | | | | | × | × |
| Make eñe word clouds | | | | | × | | | | | | | × | × | |
| **Explore the history of the eñe** | | × | | | | | | | | | | | × | × |
| **Discuss the tilde in logos**** | | | | | | | | | | × | | × | × | × |
| **Discuss the eñe as art**** | | | | | | | | | | × | | | × | × |
| **Gabriel García Márquez defends the eñe** | | | | | | | | | × | | | | × | × |
| **Hear the th**** | | | | | | × | | | | | | × | × | × |
| Highlight the range of en | | | | | × | | | | | | | × | × | |
| Exploit the -ra/-se contrast | | | | | × | | | | | | | | | × |
| Use the major past tenses | | | | | × | | | | | | | | | × |

(Continued)

| | Type of activity | | | | | | | | | | | Spanish level | | |
|---|---|---|---|---|---|---|---|---|---|---|---|---|---|---|
| | Activate knowledge | Analyze | Debate | Discuss | Create | Listen | Practice | Categorize | Read/discuss | See/discuss | Watch/discuss | Beginning | Intermediate | Advanced |
| Represent the major past tenses | ⋮ | ⋮ | ⋮ | ⋮ | × | ⋮ | ⋮ | ⋮ | ⋮ | ⋮ | ⋮ | ⋮ | ⋮ | × |
| **Discuss nosotras-themed literature, events, or slogans**** | ⋮ | ⋮ | ⋮ | ⋮ | ⋮ | ⋮ | ⋮ | ⋮ | ⋮ | × | ⋮ | ⋮ | × | × |
| Write a poem on the theme of nosotras or vosotras* | ⋮ | ⋮ | ⋮ | ⋮ | × | ⋮ | ⋮ | ⋮ | ⋮ | ⋮ | ⋮ | × | × | × |
| **Design a nosotras.com website*** | ⋮ | ⋮ | ⋮ | ⋮ | × | ⋮ | ⋮ | ⋮ | ⋮ | ⋮ | ⋮ | ⋮ | × | × |
| Design a book cover for a nosotras-themed book* | ⋮ | ⋮ | ⋮ | ⋮ | × | ⋮ | ⋮ | ⋮ | ⋮ | ⋮ | ⋮ | × | × | × |
| **Propose a nosotras-based event*** | ⋮ | ⋮ | ⋮ | ⋮ | × | ⋮ | ⋮ | ⋮ | ⋮ | ⋮ | ⋮ | ⋮ | × | × |
| **Chapter 2** | | | | | | | | | | | | | | |
| **Highlight Spanish/English capitalization differences** | ⋮ | ⋮ | ⋮ | ⋮ | × | ⋮ | ⋮ | ⋮ | ⋮ | ⋮ | ⋮ | × | × | ⋮ |
| Compare Spanish and English vowels | ⋮ | × | ⋮ | ⋮ | ⋮ | ⋮ | ⋮ | ⋮ | ⋮ | ⋮ | ⋮ | × | × | ⋮ |
| Articulate the Spanish vowel triangle | ⋮ | ⋮ | ⋮ | ⋮ | ⋮ | ⋮ | × | ⋮ | ⋮ | ⋮ | ⋮ | × | × | ⋮ |
| Analyze palabras panvocálicas | ⋮ | × | ⋮ | ⋮ | × | ⋮ | ⋮ | ⋮ | ⋮ | ⋮ | ⋮ | ⋮ | × | × |
| Tally syllable types | ⋮ | × | ⋮ | ⋮ | × | ⋮ | ⋮ | ⋮ | ⋮ | ⋮ | ⋮ | ⋮ | ⋮ | × |
| Compare Spanish and English word lengths | ⋮ | × | ⋮ | ⋮ | ⋮ | ⋮ | ⋮ | ⋮ | ⋮ | ⋮ | ⋮ | ⋮ | × | ⋮ |
| Hear the trilled r in other languages | ⋮ | ⋮ | ⋮ | ⋮ | ⋮ | × | ⋮ | ⋮ | ⋮ | ⋮ | ⋮ | × | × | × |
| Trace the development of the Spanish 'you' pronouns | ⋮ | ⋮ | ⋮ | ⋮ | ⋮ | ⋮ | ⋮ | ⋮ | ⋮ | × | ⋮ | ⋮ | × | × |
| Argue for or against multiple 'you' pronouns | ⋮ | ⋮ | × | ⋮ | × | ⋮ | ⋮ | ⋮ | ⋮ | ⋮ | ⋮ | ⋮ | ⋮ | × |
| **Choose tú or usted in a business context** | ⋮ | ⋮ | ⋮ | ⋮ | ⋮ | ⋮ | ⋮ | ⋮ | ⋮ | ⋮ | ⋮ | ⋮ | × | × |
| **Wear a tie to practice tú and usted** | ⋮ | ⋮ | ⋮ | ⋮ | ⋮ | ⋮ | × | ⋮ | ⋮ | ⋮ | ⋮ | × | × | × |
| **Link frequency and irregularity** | ⋮ | × | ⋮ | ⋮ | ⋮ | ⋮ | ⋮ | ⋮ | ⋮ | ⋮ | ⋮ | ⋮ | × | × |
| Think about irregular verbs | ⋮ | ⋮ | ⋮ | ⋮ | ⋮ | ⋮ | ⋮ | ⋮ | ⋮ | × | ⋮ | ⋮ | ⋮ | × |

| Activity | | | | | | | | | | | | | | | |
|---|---|---|---|---|---|---|---|---|---|---|---|---|---|---|---|
| **Write preterite/imperfect narratives** | | | | × | | | | | | | | | | × | × |
| Demonstrate the ubiquity of gender | | × | | | | | | | | | | | | | × |
| **Use gender-distinguished word pairs** | | | | × | | | | | | | | | | × | × |
| Explore the role of gender in fruit and tree names | | | | × | | | | | | | | | | × | × |
| Discuss or debate gender-neutral language | | | | | × | | | | | | | | | | × |
| *Chapter 3* | | | | | | | | | | | | | | | |
| **Trace the chronology of Spanish** | × | | | | | | | | | | | × | | × | × |
| Identify Indo-European languages | × | | | | | | | | | | | | | × | × |
| Group languages based on the numbers 1–10 | | × | | | | | | | | | | | × | × | × |
| Infer Indo-European culture | | | | | | | | | | × | | | | | × |
| Surprise students with pre-Roman vocabulary | × | | | | | | | | | | | | | × | × |
| Categorize pre-Roman vocabulary | | | | | | | | × | | | | | | × | × |
| Guesstimate the boundaries of the Roman Empire | × | | | | | | | | | | | × | | × | × |
| Who can name the most Romance languages? | × | | | | | | | | | | | × | | × | × |
| Identify Romance languages | × | | | | | | | | | | | × | | × | × |
| Brainstorm sources of evidence for Vulgar Latin | × | | | | | | | | | | | | | × | × |
| Categorize Germanic vocabulary | | | | | | | | × | | | | | | × | × |
| Categorize Arabic vocabulary | | | | | | | | × | | | | | | × | × |
| Arabic or not? | × | | | | | | | | | | | | | | × |
| **Observe the spread of castellano via animation** | | | | | | | | | | | × | × | × | | × |
| **Learn from a conquista quiz*** | × | | | | | | | | | | × | | | × | × |
| Explore Spanish/English borrowings | × | | | | | | | | | | | | | × | × |
| Trace changes in words | | | × | | | | | | | | | | | | × |
| Preview Spanish in the Appendix Probi | | | × | | | | | | | | | | | | × |
| Rank the sources of Spanish words | × | | | | | | | | | | | | | × | × |
| Identify doublets | | | × | | | | | | | | | | | | × |

*(Continued)*

| | Type of activity | | | | | | | | | | | Spanish level | | |
|---|---|---|---|---|---|---|---|---|---|---|---|---|---|---|
| | Activate knowledge | Analyze | Debate | Discuss | Create | Listen | Practice | Categorize | Read/discuss | See/discuss | Watch/discuss | Beginning | Intermediate | Advanced |
| **Match borrowed words with their sources** | × | | | | | | | | | | | | × | × |
| Predict the origins of borrowed words | × | | | | | | | | | | | | × | × |
| Find semantic patterns in borrowed words | | | | | | | | | | | | | × | × |
| Categorize changes in meaning | | | | | | | | × | | | | | | × |
| **Identify directional aspects of *para* uses** | | | | | | | | | | × | | | × | × |
| Brainstorm descendants of *ille* | | × | | | | | | | | | | | | × |
| Match Spanish conjugations to Latin | | × | | | | | | | | | | | | × |
| Look for differences between stem-changing and regular verbs | | × | | | | | | | | | | × | × | × |
| **Categorize stem-changing verbs** | | × | | | | | | | | | | × | × | × |
| Discover the multiple sources of *ser* and *ir* | | × | | × | | | | | | | | | | × |
| Consider the Latin case system and its disappearance | | | | × | | | | | | | | | | × |
| *Chapter 4* | | | | | | | | | | | | | | |
| Brainstorm about language variation | | | | × | | | | | | | | | | × |
| **Discuss dialects in general** | × | | | × | | | | | | | | | | × |
| Listen to examples of different dialects | | | | | | × | | | | | | | × | × |
| **Map minority languages** | × | | | | | | | | | | | | × | × |
| Listen to minority languages | | | | | | × | | | | | | | × | × |
| Read a Catalan text | | | | | | | × | | | | | | | × |
| **Discuss the language section of the Spanish Constitution** | | | | | | | | | × | | | | | × |

| Activity | | | | | | | | | | | | | | | |
|---|---|---|---|---|---|---|---|---|---|---|---|---|---|---|---|
| **Discuss the language controversy in Catalonian schools** | ⋮ | ⋮ | ⋮ | ⋮ | ⋮ | ⋮ | ⋮ | ⋮ | ⋮ | x | ⋮ | ⋮ | ⋮ | ⋮ | x | x |
| Estimate or interpret basic statistics about indigenous languages | x | ⋮ | ⋮ | ⋮ | ⋮ | ⋮ | ⋮ | ⋮ | ⋮ | ⋮ | ⋮ | ⋮ | x | x | x | x |
| **Compare indigenous languages in Latin America and the United States** | ⋮ | ⋮ | ⋮ | ⋮ | ⋮ | ⋮ | ⋮ | ⋮ | x | ⋮ | x | x | x | x | x | x |
| Listen to indigenous languages** | ⋮ | ⋮ | ⋮ | ⋮ | x | ⋮ | ⋮ | ⋮ | ⋮ | ⋮ | ⋮ | ⋮ | x | x | x | x |
| **Discuss the challenges of immigration for indigenous language speakers** | ⋮ | ⋮ | ⋮ | ⋮ | ⋮ | ⋮ | ⋮ | x | ⋮ | x | ⋮ | ⋮ | x | x | x | x |
| Discuss the constitutional status of indigenous languages** | ⋮ | ⋮ | ⋮ | ⋮ | ⋮ | ⋮ | x | ⋮ | ⋮ | ⋮ | ⋮ | ⋮ | ⋮ | ⋮ | ⋮ | x |
| Speak indigenous-influenced Spanish | ⋮ | ⋮ | ⋮ | ⋮ | ⋮ | ⋮ | ⋮ | ⋮ | ⋮ | ⋮ | ⋮ | ⋮ | ⋮ | x | x | x |
| **Observe the installation of Evo Morales** | ⋮ | ⋮ | ⋮ | ⋮ | ⋮ | ⋮ | ⋮ | ⋮ | ⋮ | x | ⋮ | ⋮ | x | x | x | x |
| **Code-switch between Spanish and English** | ⋮ | ⋮ | ⋮ | ⋮ | ⋮ | ⋮ | x | ⋮ | x | ⋮ | ⋮ | ⋮ | ⋮ | x | x | x |
| Ask questions using Paraguayan code-switching | ⋮ | ⋮ | ⋮ | ⋮ | ⋮ | ⋮ | ⋮ | x | x | ⋮ | ⋮ | ⋮ | ⋮ | ⋮ | ⋮ | x |
| Analyze Andalusian wall plaques | ⋮ | ⋮ | ⋮ | ⋮ | ⋮ | ⋮ | ⋮ | ⋮ | ⋮ | ⋮ | x | ⋮ | ⋮ | x | x | x |
| **Listen to final s** | ⋮ | ⋮ | ⋮ | ⋮ | ⋮ | ⋮ | x | ⋮ | ⋮ | ⋮ | ⋮ | ⋮ | ⋮ | x | x | x |
| Discuss factors in variation | ⋮ | ⋮ | ⋮ | x | ⋮ | ⋮ | ⋮ | ⋮ | ⋮ | ⋮ | ⋮ | ⋮ | ⋮ | ⋮ | ⋮ | x |
| **Listen to yeísmo** | ⋮ | ⋮ | ⋮ | ⋮ | ⋮ | ⋮ | x | ⋮ | ⋮ | ⋮ | ⋮ | ⋮ | ⋮ | x | x | x |
| Practice seseo, ceceo, and the s/th contrast with tongue twisters | ⋮ | ⋮ | ⋮ | ⋮ | ⋮ | ⋮ | ⋮ | ⋮ | ⋮ | ⋮ | ⋮ | ⋮ | ⋮ | ⋮ | x | x |
| Listen to -ao and -ío | ⋮ | ⋮ | ⋮ | ⋮ | ⋮ | ⋮ | x | ⋮ | ⋮ | ⋮ | ⋮ | x | ⋮ | x | x | x |
| Debate the linguistic relevance of mass media | ⋮ | ⋮ | x | ⋮ | ⋮ | ⋮ | ⋮ | ⋮ | ⋮ | ⋮ | ⋮ | ⋮ | ⋮ | ⋮ | ⋮ | x |
| Listen to the Puerto Rican r | ⋮ | ⋮ | ⋮ | ⋮ | ⋮ | ⋮ | x | ⋮ | ⋮ | ⋮ | ⋮ | ⋮ | ⋮ | ⋮ | ⋮ | x |
| **Compare perspectives on the Puerto Rican r** | ⋮ | ⋮ | ⋮ | ⋮ | ⋮ | ⋮ | ⋮ | ⋮ | ⋮ | x | ⋮ | ⋮ | ⋮ | ⋮ | x | x |
| Maintain a word board or map | x | ⋮ | ⋮ | ⋮ | ⋮ | x | ⋮ | ⋮ | ⋮ | ⋮ | ⋮ | ⋮ | x | x | x | x |
| **Use dialectal vocabulary** | ⋮ | ⋮ | ⋮ | ⋮ | ⋮ | x | ⋮ | ⋮ | ⋮ | ⋮ | ⋮ | ⋮ | ⋮ | x | x | x |
| Answer questions with (or without) leísmo | ⋮ | ⋮ | ⋮ | ⋮ | ⋮ | ⋮ | ⋮ | x | ⋮ | ⋮ | ⋮ | ⋮ | ⋮ | ⋮ | ⋮ | x |
| Examine changing standards for object pronouns | ⋮ | ⋮ | ⋮ | ⋮ | ⋮ | x | ⋮ | ⋮ | ⋮ | ⋮ | ⋮ | ⋮ | ⋮ | ⋮ | x | x |
| Infer nationalities from dialogues | ⋮ | ⋮ | ⋮ | ⋮ | ⋮ | ⋮ | ⋮ | ⋮ | ⋮ | ⋮ | ⋮ | ⋮ | ⋮ | x | x | x |
| **Discuss readings on voseo and tuteo** | ⋮ | ⋮ | ⋮ | ⋮ | ⋮ | ⋮ | ⋮ | ⋮ | ⋮ | x | ⋮ | ⋮ | ⋮ | ⋮ | x | x |

(Continued)

|  | Type of activity |  |  |  |  |  |  |  |  |  |  | Spanish level |  |  |
|---|---|---|---|---|---|---|---|---|---|---|---|---|---|---|
|  | Activate knowledge | Analyze | Debate | Discuss | Create | Listen | Practice | Categorize | Read/discuss | See/discuss | Watch/discuss | Beginning | Intermediate | Advanced |
| Observe intimate Colombian *usted* |  |  |  |  |  |  |  |  | × |  |  |  | × | × |
| **Interpret non-standard verb forms** |  |  |  |  |  |  |  |  |  | × |  |  |  | × |
| *Chapter 5* |  |  |  |  |  |  |  |  |  |  |  |  |  |  |
| Analyze words from motherese |  | × |  |  |  |  |  |  |  |  |  |  | × | × |
| Observe motherese videos |  |  |  |  |  |  |  |  |  |  | × |  | × | × |
| Predict the order of acquisition of consonants | × |  |  |  |  |  |  |  |  |  |  |  | × | × |
| Predict children's first words | × |  |  |  |  |  |  |  |  |  |  |  | × | × |
| Categorize children's first words |  |  |  |  |  |  |  | × |  |  |  |  | × | × |
| **Analyze children's semantic overextensions** |  | × |  |  |  |  |  |  |  |  |  |  | × | × |
| Predict children's first uses of *por, para, ser,* and *estar* | × |  |  |  |  |  |  |  |  |  |  |  |  | × |
| Contrast L1 and L2 learning of *por* and other prepositions |  |  |  |  |  |  |  |  | × | × |  |  | × | × |
| Think about gender acquisition |  |  |  | × |  |  |  |  |  |  |  |  |  | × |
| **Analyze children's gender errors*** |  | × |  |  |  |  |  |  |  |  |  |  | × | × |
| Spot tenses in videos of children speaking Spanish |  |  |  |  | × |  |  |  |  |  | × |  | × | × |
| Analyze the order of acquisition of verb tenses |  | × |  |  |  |  |  |  |  |  |  |  |  | × |
| **Analyze children's conjugation errors** |  | × |  |  |  |  |  |  |  |  |  |  | × | × |
| Think about the verb acquisition process |  |  |  | × |  |  |  |  |  |  |  |  |  | × |
| Reflect on second language learning |  |  |  | × |  |  |  |  |  |  |  | × | × | × |
| **Brainstorm on applications of learning styles** |  |  |  |  |  |  |  |  |  |  |  | × | × | × |
| Self-profile the student as a language learner | × |  |  |  |  |  |  |  |  |  |  | × |  | × |
| **Interpret speech errors** |  | × |  |  |  |  |  |  |  |  |  |  | × | × |
| **Practice a *jerigonza*** |  |  |  |  |  |  | × |  |  |  |  |  | × | × |

# Take-home projects

This appendix characterizes the sixty-seven take-home projects described in this book by their type (as listed in Table 3 in the Introduction) and appropriate level of Spanish. Many activities are appropriate for more than one level of Spanish or can be adapted to more than one level, as discussed in the Introduction.

Also as described in the Introduction, projects in boldface are of sufficient interest that teachers should consider using them in their classes even if they do not adopt the book's essential questions curriculum more broadly.

Projects marked with a double asterisk (**) supplement or replace a corresponding in-class activity.

| | Type of project | | | | | | | | | Spanish level | | |
|---|---|---|---|---|---|---|---|---|---|---|---|---|
| | Ask a native speaker | Collect and analyze data | Create | Find example(s) | Look up items | Research | Profile | Try something new | WebQuest | Beginning | Intermediate | Advanced |
| **Chapter 1** | | | | | | | | | | | | |
| Profile a Spanish-speaking country | | | | | | | x | | | x | | |
| Profile a Spanish language Academy | | | | | | | x | | | | x | |
| Profile an Academy's members | | | | | | | x | | | | x | x |
| Prepare interview questions for an Academy member | | | x | | | | | | | | x | x |
| **Profile a Nobel Prize winner** | | | | | | | x | | | | x | |
| **Argue for or against the inverted marks** | | | x | | | | | | | | | x |
| **Create a class logo** | | | x | | | | | | | x | | |
| Trace eñe etymologies | | | | | x | | | | | | x | x |
| **Explore the tilde in logos and art**** | | | x | | | | | | | | x | x |
| **Find th examples**** | | | | x | | | | | | | x | x |
| **Trace the takeover of the -ra subjunctive** | | x | | | | | | | | | | x |
| Quantify past tense usage | | x | | | | | | | | | | x |
| **Explore nosotras in literature, events, or politics**** | | | x | | | | | | | | x | x |
| Ask a native speaker about nosotras | x | | | | | | | | | x | x | x |
| **Chapter 2** | | | | | | | | | | | | |
| Write a story with palabras panvocálicas | | | x | | | | | | | | | x |
| **Tackle the trilled r** | | | | | | | | x | | x | x | x |
| WebQuest: Explore the history of estar | | | | | | | | | x | | | x |
| **Ask a native speaker about their pronoun usage** | x | | | | | | | | | x | x | x |

| Project | C1 | C2 | C3 | C4 | C5 | C6 | C7 | C8 | C9 | C10 | C11 | C12 | C13 | C14 |
|---|---|---|---|---|---|---|---|---|---|---|---|---|---|---|
| **Test preterite/imperfect guidelines** | | X | | | | | | | | | | | X | X |
| Compare noun genders in Spanish and another language | | X | | | | | | | | | | | X | X |
| **Research gender-neutral Spanish** | | | | | | X | | | | | | | | X |
| Push the boundaries of the personal *a* | | | | X | | | | | | | | | X | X |
| **Write a quiz using ¿Quién(es)? and ¿A quién(es)?** | | X | | | | | | | | | | | X | X |
| *Chapter 3* | | | | | | | | | | | | | | |
| **Create a class timeline of the history of Spanish** | | X | | | | | | | | | X | | X | X |
| **Color-code a map of the Indo-European region** | | | | | | | X | | | | X | | X | X |
| Research pre-Roman place names | | | | | | | X | | | | | | X | X |
| Research Romance demographics | | | | | | | X | | | | | | X | |
| Profile a Romance language | | | | | | | | X | | | | | X | X |
| Compare *castellano* to other European language standards | | | | | | | X | | | | | | | X |
| **Research New World etymologies** | | | | | | | X | | | | | | X | X |
| Identify new-ish Spanish words | | | X | | | | | | | | | | X | X |
| Research the origins of words from a semantic domain | | X | | | | | | | | | X | | X | X |
| Research the origins of words in a text | | X | | | | | X | | | | | | X | |
| **Greek or not Greek?** | | | | | | | X | | | | X | | | X |
| **Trace the growth of the -ir a future** | | | | | | X | | | | | X | | X | X |
| Identify original -zco verbs | | | | | | | X | | | | | | X | |
| *Chapter 4* | | | | | | | | | | | | | | |
| **Profile a dialect** | | | | | | | | | X | | | | X | X |
| Profile a country's dialect(s) | | | | | | | | | X | | | | X | X |
| Learn from "dialectos del español" videos | | | X | | | | | | | | | | X | X |
| **Ask a native speaker about dialects** | X | | | | | | | | X | | | | X | X |
| **Profile a minority language** | | | | | | | | | X | | | | X | X |

*(Continued)*

| | Type of project | | | | | | | | | Spanish level | | |
|---|---|---|---|---|---|---|---|---|---|---|---|---|
| | Ask a native speaker | Collect and analyze data | Create | Find example(s) | Look up items | Research | Profile | Try something new | WebQuest | Beginning | Intermediate | Advanced |
| **Compare the Catalan/Castilian conflict to another language conflict** | | | | | | × | | | | | | × |
| WebQuest: Explore advocacy groups | | | | | | | | | × | | | × |
| **What's new with minority languages?** | | | | | | × | | | | | | × |
| **WebQuest about indigenous languages** | | | | | | | | | × | | × | × |
| Profile an indigenous language | | | | | | | × | | | | × | × |
| Find a video of an indigenous language** | | | | × | | | | | | | × | × |
| **Map the most-spoken indigenous languages** | | | | | × | | | | | × | × | |
| Research language status in Latin American constitutions** | | | | | × | | | | | | | × |
| Ask a native speaker about s deletion | × | | | | | | | | | | × | × |
| **Find examples of yeísmo (or the y/ll contrast)** | | | | × | | | | | | | | × |
| Trace dialectal variants to their countries | | | | | × | | | | | | × | × |
| **Find dialectal variants for a list of meanings** | | | | | × | | | | | × | × | × |
| Find dialectal vocabulary via the Internet | | | | × | | | | | | × | × | × |
| **Ask a native speaker about vocabulary from their country** | × | | | | | | | | | × | × | × |
| **Ask a native speaker about dialectal pronoun differences** | × | | | | | | | | | × | × | × |
| Ask a native speaker about future tense usage | × | | | | | | | | | | × | × |

| *Chapter 5* | | | | | | | | | | | |
|---|---|---|---|---|---|---|---|---|---|---|---|
| Ask a native speaker about motherese | X | ⋮ | ⋮ | ⋮ | ⋮ | ⋮ | ⋮ | ⋮ | ⋮ | ⋮ | X |
| **Observe a two-year-old's speech** | ⋮ | X | ⋮ | ⋮ | ⋮ | ⋮ | ⋮ | ⋮ | ⋮ | X | X |
| **Ask a native speaker about children's conjugation errors** | X | ⋮ | ⋮ | ⋮ | ⋮ | ⋮ | ⋮ | ⋮ | X | X | X |
| **Try a sample online Spanish lesson** | ⋮ | ⋮ | ⋮ | ⋮ | ⋮ | ⋮ | X | ⋮ | X | X | X |
| Tackle listening comprehension | ⋮ | ⋮ | ⋮ | ⋮ | X | ⋮ | ⋮ | ⋮ | X | X | X |
| Compare Spooner and Pich i Pon | ⋮ | ⋮ | ⋮ | ⋮ | ⋮ | ⋮ | ⋮ | X | ⋮ | X | X |
| Reproduce a grammatical gender experiment | ⋮ | ⋮ | ⋮ | ⋮ | X | ⋮ | ⋮ | ⋮ | ⋮ | ⋮ | X |
| **Find a meme for the *se accidental*** | ⋮ | ⋮ | X | ⋮ | ⋮ | ⋮ | ⋮ | ⋮ | ⋮ | ⋮ | X |
| Prepare a *jerigonza* dialogue | ⋮ | ⋮ | ⋮ | ⋮ | ⋮ | ⋮ | X | ⋮ | ⋮ | X | X |
| Ask a native speaker about *jerigonzas* | X | ⋮ | ⋮ | ⋮ | ⋮ | ⋮ | ⋮ | ⋮ | ⋮ | X | X |

# Appendix C

# Slides

Note: As discussed in the Introduction, slides with titles **in boldface** are (in the author's judgment) most likely to be useful to any Spanish teacher, whether or not they follow the overall program in this book.

1   How is Spanish different from other languages?

    1.1    Los 10 idiomas más hablados del mundo
    1.2    Veintiún países de habla española oficial
    1.3    Los 10 idiomas más hablados del mundo (en orden alfabético)
    1.4    Veintidós países de habla hispana (en orden alfabético)
    **1.5    Los 5 países más hispanohablantes del mundo**
    1.6    ¿Dónde viven los hispanohablantes?
    1.7    Veintidós países de habla hispana y sus hablantes de español como primer idioma
    1.8    Un perfil lingüístico de un país hispanohablante
    1.9    Video: "300 años de la Real Academia Española" (3:19)
    1.10    Video: "La casa de las palabras" (5:41)
    1.11    Dos temas de debate posibles sobre la Real Academia Española
    1.12    La Real Academia Española explica la eliminación de *ch* y *ll*
    1.13    La eliminación de *ch* y *ll*: ventajas y desventajas
    1.14    Hugo Chávez se burla de la eliminación de la letra *ch*
    1.15    Un perfil de una academia de la lengua española
    1.16    Un perfil de los miembros de una academia de la lengua española
    **1.17    Ganadores hispanos del Premio Nobel de Literatura**
    1.18    ¿De dónde son los ganadores hispanos del Premio Nobel de Literatura?
    1.19    Fotos oficiales de los ganadores hispanos del Premio Nobel de Literatura
    1.20    Un perfil de un ganador hispano del Premio Nobel de Literatura
    **1.21    La invención de las marcas invertidas ¿ y ¡**
    1.22    ?Quien me llama? !que misericordioso es Dios!
    1.23    Temas de debate sobre la invención de las marcas ¿ y ¡

# Index

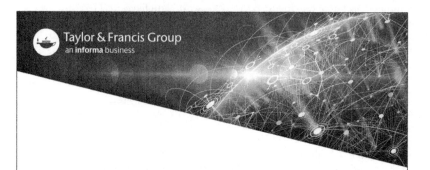